Comfort and
Holiness from Christ's
Priestly Work

SERIES EDITORS
Joel R. Beeke & Jay T. Collier

Interest in the Puritans continues to grow, but many people find the reading of these giants of the faith a bit unnerving. This series seeks to overcome that barrier by presenting Puritan books that are convenient in size and unintimidating in length. Each book is carefully edited with modern readers in mind, smoothing out difficult language of a bygone era while retaining the meaning of the original authors. Books for the series are thoughtfully selected to provide some of the best counsel on important subjects that people continue to wrestle with today.

Comfort and Holiness from Christ's Priestly Work

William Bridge

Edited by
Brian G. Hedges

Reformation Heritage Books
Grand Rapids, Michigan

Reformation Heritage Books
2965 Leonard St. NE
Grand Rapids, MI 49525
616-977-0889
orders@heritagebooks.org
www.heritagebooks.org

Originally published in 1647 as *The Great Gospel Mystery of the Saint's Comfort and Holiness, Opened and Applied from Christ's Priestly Office.*

Unless otherwise indicated, Scripture is taken from the New King James Version®. Copyright © 1982 by Thomas Nelson. Used by permission. All rights reserved.

Scripture marked KJV is taken from the King James Version.

Printed in the United States of America
19 20 21 22 23 24/10 9 8 7 6 5 4 3 2 1

Library of Congress Cataloging-in-Publication Data

Names: Bridge, William, 1600 or 1601-1671, author. | Hedges, Brian G., editor.
Title: Comfort and holiness from Christ's priestly work / William Bridge ; edited by Brian G. Hedges.
Description: Grand Rapids, Michigan : Reformation Heritage Books, 2019. | Includes bibliographical references.
Identifiers: LCCN 2019041142 (print) | LCCN 2019041143 (ebook) | ISBN 9781601787231 (paperback) | ISBN 9781601787248 (epub)
Subjects: LCSH: Jesus Christ—Priesthood.
Classification: LCC BT254 .B75 2019 (print) | LCC BT254 (ebook) | DDC 232/.8—dc23
LC record available at https://lccn.loc.gov/2019041142
LC ebook record available at https://lccn.loc.gov/2019041143

For additional Reformed literature, request a free book list from Reformation Heritage Books at the above regular or e-mail address.

Table of Contents

Preface

The message of this book is that "Christ's office as a priest is the great storehouse and supply of all the grace and comfort that we have on this side of heaven." If true, nothing is more vital to a believer's comfort and sanctification than understanding the scope of our Lord's priestly office. Conversely, if you are struggling with sin, doubt, temptation, discouragement, or an accusing conscience, the reason may well be that you've never grasped the significance of Christ's priesthood.

The first person to draw distinctive attention to Christ's threefold office as prophet, priest, and king, was Eusebius in his *Church History*.[1] But this rich biblical terrain wasn't really mapped and explored until the Reformation. In his *Institutes*, Calvin said, "In order that

---

1. Eusebius, *Church History*, 1.3.8, in *Nicene and Post-Nicene Fathers*, ed. Phillip Schaff and Henry Wace (New York: Christian Literature, 1890; repr., Peabody, Mass.: Hendrickson, 2004), 1:85–87.

faith may find a firm basis for salvation in Christ, and thus rest in him, this principle must be laid down: the office enjoined upon Christ by the Father consists of three parts. For he was given to be prophet, king, and priest."[2] Calvin then expounded Christ's priestly office, focusing on its two aspects of reconciliation and intercession.[3]

In rejecting the priesthood of the Roman Catholic Church, the Reformers inaugurated a period of renewed focus on the mediatorial work of Christ as our Great High Priest—the centrality of which is reflected in the confessional standards of various Reformed churches.[4]

The Puritans brought this focus on Christ's priestly work to its zenith in their sermons and treatises, exploring in surpassing detail and depth the full scope of His sacerdotal office.[5] One of the best examples is found in an

---

2. John Calvin, *Institutes of the Christian Religion*, ed. John T. McNeill, trans. Ford Lewis Battles (Philadelphia: Westminster, 1960), 2.15.1.

3. Calvin, *Institutes*, 2.15.6.

4. For example, see Belgic Confession of Faith, art. 21, 26; Heidelberg Catechism 31; Westminster Confession of Faith 8; and Westminster Shorter Catechism 23–26.

5. For example, see John Flavel, *The Fountain of Life Opened Up, or, A Display of Christ in His Essential and Mediatorial Glory*, in *The Works of John Flavel* (London: W. Baynes and Son, 1820; repr., Edinburgh: Banner of Truth Trust, 1968), 1:32–561; Thomas Goodwin, *Christ Set Forth*, in *The Works of Thomas Goodwin* (Edinburgh: James Nichol, 1861; repr., Eureka, Calif.: Tanski, 1996), 4:1–91; Goodwin, *The Heart of Christ in Heaven Towards Sinners on Earth*, in *Works*, 4:93–150; John Owen, Salus Electorum,

almost forgotten series of sermons preached in Stepney, England, by William Bridge in 1647, originally entitled *The Great Gospel Mystery of the Saint's Comfort and Holiness, Opened and Applied from Christ's Priestly Office.*

Who Was William Bridge?

Born in Cambridgeshire, England, in 1600 and educated at Emmanuel College in Cambridge, William Bridge became one of the leading nonconformist ministers in the mid-seventeenth century.[6] After earning a bachelor's degree in 1623 and a master of arts degree in 1626, Bridge was ordained as a priest in the Church of England in 1627. He became the rector of St. Peter Hungate in Norwich in 1632 but was scrutinized in 1634 for affirming limited atonement and condemning Arminianism. Following a temporary suspension, he returned to ministry only to be silenced and excommunicated by Bishop Matthew Wren two years later, in 1636. Banished from England, Bridge fled to Holland, where he took up

---

Sanguis Jesui; *or, The Death of Death in the Death of Christ,* in *The Works of John Owen,* ed. W. H. Goold (Edinburgh: 1850–53; repr., Edinburgh: Banner of Truth Trust, 1966), 10:139–479; and John Owen, *Exercitations on the Epistle to the Hebrews, Part IV: Concerning the Sacerdotal Office of Christ,* in *Works,* 18:1–259.

6. For biographical information, I've relied on Joel Beeke and Randall J. Pederson, *Meet the Puritans: With a Guide to Modern Reprints* (Grand Rapids: Reformation Heritage Books, 2007), 92–95; and H. Rondel Rumburg, *William Bridge: The Puritan of the Congregational Way* (n.p.: Xulon Press, 2003).

residence in Rotterdam, renounced his ordination in the Church of England, and began his labors as an Independent. Concerning Bridge's exile, Archbishop Laud wrote to Charles I: "But in Norwhich, one Mr. Bridge, rather than he will conform, hath left his Lecture and two Cures, and is gone to Holland." The king tersely commented, "Let him go, we are well rid of him!"[7]

Bridge soon joined hands with other refugees in Holland. He was ordained by John Ward, the stepson of Richard Rogers. Bridge in turn ordained Ward, and they began laboring together. During his years in Rotterdam, Bridge also worked closely with Jeremiah Burroughs, another of the great Independent ministers of the day.

In 1641 Bridge was able to return to England. During the next two decades, he exercised considerable political and ecclesiastical influence. He frequently addressed the Long Parliament (1640–1660), preaching to both the House of Commons and House of Lords. In 1642 he was appointed to be a member of the Westminster Assembly.[8] In an effort to promote congregational

---

7. Rumburg, *William Bridge: The Puritan of the Congregational Way*, 74–75.

8. Bridge was one of only ten Independent divines who sat in the Assembly. The others were Philip Nye, Thomas Goodwin, Jeremiah Burroughs, William Greenhill, John Phillip, Peter Sterry, Joseph Caryl, William Carter, and Sidrach Simpson. See Rumburg, *William Bridge*, 118.

church government, he coauthored *An Apologetical Narration*.[9] Along with John Owen and Thomas Goodwin, Bridge was also one of the six divines involved in drawing up the Savoy Declaration (1658), a congregational confession modeled after the Westminster Confession of Faith.[10] He also helped establish a congregational church in Yarmouth in 1643, laboring among the people until the Act of Uniformity in 1662, when he was among two thousand ministers who were ejected from the pulpit. He died in Clapham on March 12, 1670.

Among readers of Puritan literature today, William Bridge is probably best known for his thirteen sermons on Psalm 42:11, entitled *A Lifting Up for the Downcast*, published in Banner of Truth's Puritan Paperback series in 1961. Such was my introduction to Bridge. And I was so greatly helped that I sought out and was thrilled to obtain a set of his five-volume *Works*. The book now in your hands is a modernization of Bridge's four sermons on Christ's priestly work.[11]

---

9. The other authors were Jeremiah Burroughs, Thomas Goodwin, Philip Nye, and Sidrach Simpson.

10. The others were Philip Nye, Joseph Caryl, and William Greenhill.

11. William Bridge, *The Great Gospel Mystery of the Saints' Comfort and Holiness, Opened and Applied from Christ's Priestly Office*, in *The Works of the Rev. William Bridge, M. A.* (Thomas Kegg, 1845; repr., Beaver Falls, Penn.: Soli Deo Gloria, 1989), 1:1–85.

The Persuasive Pleader

Few preachers have been more helpful to me than William Bridge. His preaching is marked by two qualities that will, I believe, prove to be a blessing to other readers as well.

Bridge Was an Experiential Preacher

The theologian and professor John Murray, while driving with a friend in northern Scotland, asked, "What is the difference between a lecture and preaching?" His friend, unable to give a satisfactory response, asked the professor to answer his own question. Murray replied, "This is what it is: Preaching is a personal passionate plea."[12] That well describes the preaching of William Bridge. His heartfelt sermons directly address the spiritual experiences of believers.

You will sense this as you read Bridge, especially as he tackled the doubts, fears, and objections of his people. In the course of addressing such concerns, Bridge both argued and pleaded. He argued against the objections hearers might raise in their own minds that would keep them from taking comfort in the promises of the gospel, and he pleaded with them to respond with faith.

12. Alistair Begg and Sinclair B. Ferguson, *Name above All Names* (Wheaton, Ill.: Crossway, 2013), 48.

Readers will especially note Bridge's pathos by his frequent use of the exclamative "Oh!"[13]

Robert Halley in his *Memoir of Thomas Goodwin*, commenting on Independents in the Westminster Assembly, said that Goodwin was their leader, "Nye was a powerful speaker, Burroughs an astute reasoner, [and] Bridge a persuasive pleader."[14] Bridge powerfully exemplified this pleading quality in his sermons—a quality all too absent in many pulpits today. His messages not

---

13. The sermons of Bridge display a remarkable balance of what John Carrick has called "sacred rhetoric" in the use of the indicative, exclamative, interrogative, and imperative moods. Carrick shows how Scripture itself provides the pattern of rhetoric. "True preaching, then, always involves a balance between the *indicative* and the *imperative*. True preaching always involves *explication et applicaction verbi Dei*—it always involves the explication and application of the Word of God.... True preaching is not *mere explication*; nor is it *mere exhortation*. Explication and exhortation must co-exist in proper tension and balance." Carrick further notes "that each of the four grammatical or rhetorical categories...has its own homiletical qualities and value." The indicative appeals to the mind, which is reinforced by the exclamative, which moves the emotions; the interrogative probes the conscience, while the imperative, with its emphasis on application, appeals to the will. John Carrick, *The Imperative of Preaching: A Theology of Sacred Rhetoric* (Edinburgh: Banner of Truth Trust, 2002), 145–48. Bridge uses all four rhetorical categories but is especially notable for his use of the exclamative.

14. *Memoir of Thomas Goodwin*, in *The Works of Thomas Goodwin* (Eureka, Calif.: Tanski, 1996), 2:xviii. Quoted in Rumburg, *William Bridge: The Puritan of the Congregational Way*, 138.

only emanate light, they radiate heat. You will be both instructed and moved by reading Bridge.

Bridge Was a Christ-Centered Preacher

We could say Christ-centered preaching is a trait, of course, of almost all the Puritans. But it was especially true of William Bridge, who had what John Owen called "a secret instinct in faith, whereby it knows the voice of Christ when he speaks indeed."[15]

This Christ-centered, gospel instinct was both the overflow of Bridge's own love for the Lord Jesus Christ and the outworking of his profoundly evangelical theology. Bridge spoke with the accent of a new covenant believer who has fled from the thunderous terrors of Sinai into the arms of Jesus Christ. As you will observe in these sermons, Bridge knew his Bible well. His messages abound in insightful forays into the Old Testament Scriptures. But he read his Bible through gospel-tinted lenses.[16]

Of all the Puritans I've read, William Bridge most reminds me of Martin Luther before him (and Charles Spurgeon after him). In fact, Bridge often quoted Luther in his messages. His sermons joyfully exulted in

---

15. John Owen, *Of the Mortification of Sin in Believers*, in *Works*, 6:77.

16. For Bridge's exposition of the nature of the new covenant, see his *Christ and the Covenant*, in *The Works of the Rev. William Bridge*, 2:1–196.

the finished work of Christ, forcefully applied the fullness of Christ's work to all the exigencies of the soul, and exuded throughout the sweet fragrance of gospel holiness. His preaching revealed the tender heart of a shepherd for his sheep, as he led them into the fertile pastures of God's redemptive grace given in Christ. Nowhere is this more evident than in the sermons before you, as Bridge opened and applied "the great gospel mystery of the saints' comfort and holiness" in the priestly work of the Lord Jesus Christ.

As "a persuasive pleader," William Bridge was a very Christlike man. The apostle Paul said, "God was in Christ reconciling the world to Himself, not imputing their trespasses to them, and has committed to us the word of reconciliation," and then he said, "Now then, we are ambassadors for Christ, as though God were pleading through us: we implore you on Christ's behalf, be reconciled to God" (2 Cor. 5:19–20). The Lord Jesus is also a persuasive pleader, as He earnestly entreats us through the ministry of the preached word.

But Christ not only pleads with us, *He also pleads for us.* For this is one crucial aspect of His work as our High Priest. In His priestly office, God's beloved Son pleads persuasively for His people in the presence of His gracious Father. "Therefore He is also able to save to the uttermost those who come to God through Him, since He always lives to make intercession for them" (Heb. 7:25).

The Advocate

Almost two hundred years after William Bridge died in 1670, an Anglican Irish-American woman named Charitie Lees Smith (later Bancroft) wrote a hymn called "The Advocate." I believe Bridge would have loved this hymn, for it grounds our assurance and confidence in the finished work of our Great High Priest. It is a fitting hymn to accompany these sermons, in which, though William Bridge is dead, he still speaks.

> Before the throne of God above
> I have a strong, a perfect plea;
> A great High Priest, whose Name is Love,
> Who ever lives and pleads for me.
> My name is graven on His hands,
> My name is written on His heart;
> I know that while with God He stands
> No tongue can bid me thence depart.
>
> When Satan tempts me to despair,
> And tells me of the guilt within,
> Upward I look, and see Him there
> Who made an end of all my sin.
> Because the sinless Savior died,
> My sinful soul is counted free;
> For God, the Just, is satisfied
> To look on Him and pardon me.

Behold Him there, the risen Lamb!
My perfect, spotless Righteousness,
The great unchangeable I AM,
The King of glory and of grace.
One with Himself, I cannot die;
My soul is purchased by His blood;
My life is hid with Christ on high,
With Christ, my Savior and my God.[17]

—Brian G. Hedges
February 2019

---

17. Charitie Lees Bancroft, "The Advocate," also known as "Before the Throne of God Above," 1863, in the public domain.

Therefore, in all things He had to be made like His brethren, that He might be a merciful and faithful High Priest in things pertaining to God, to make propitiation for the sins of the people. For in that He Himself has suffered, being tempted, He is able to aid those who are tempted.

—Hebrews 2:17–18

CHAPTER 1

Christ's Priestly Work

In the earlier part of Hebrews 2, the author showed why it was fitting for Christ to suffer death. Then in the last part of this chapter, he gave an account for why it was fitting for Christ to be made like us "His brethren" in all things (v. 17).

In other scriptures we find our Lord and Savior Christ is called our Father, "Everlasting Father, Prince of Peace" (Isa. 9:6). Here He is called our brother, and we His brothers.

Now in natural human relationships, the same person cannot be both a father and a brother to the same man. But these relationships aren't sufficient metaphors for showing the love of Jesus Christ toward us. For while a father provides for his child, the child's brother does not. But a brother can stoop and condescend to his brother in a way that is not fitting to the superiority of the father. And so here we see the stooping, condescending love of Jesus Christ. That is why He is called our brother, and we are called His brethren.

But why should the Lord Jesus Christ be made like His brethren in all things? The apostle gave the reason: "Therefore, in all things He had to be made like His brethren, that He might be a merciful and faithful High Priest in things pertaining to God, to make propitiation for the sins of the people" (Heb. 2:17). The Lord God, our Father, swore to Jesus Christ, "You are a priest forever according to the order of Melchizedek" (Heb. 7:17). Christ was to be the Great High Priest. The Jews, in Old Testament times, had a high priest who in all things stood between God and the people, so that if anyone sinned, the priest could make an atonement for them. The Lord Jesus Christ is the Apostle and High Priest of our Christian profession, as Aaron was of the Jews' profession. This is why the apostle said it behooved Him to be made like us in all things.

But why couldn't Jesus Christ be merciful to poor, tempted souls, unless He were in all things made like them—in their natures, in their affections, and in their temptations? For Christ as God could have been merciful to us even if He had not been made like us. But if He wasn't like us, he couldn't have been merciful *as our High Priest*.

There is a difference between an ability of sufficiency and power on one hand, and an ability of suitability and fitness on the other. Christ, as God, has an ability of sufficiency to be able to help those who are tempted, even if He had never been tempted Himself. But the ability

of suitability and fitness—or aptness and disposition—
depends upon the nature He shared with us in His
incarnation. That is why the apostle said, "For in that He
Himself has suffered, being tempted, He is able to aid
those who are tempted" (Heb. 2:18). And that is why the
Christian's great support and source of help against all
temptations lies in the priestly office of Jesus Christ.

Christ's office as priest is the great storehouse and
supply of all the grace and comfort that we have on
this side of heaven. Through Christ's priesthood we are
reconciled to God the Father and are relieved against
all temptations. This is the great truth held forth in
this text. That's why the apostle, finding the Hebrews
laboring under great temptations, doubts, fears, and
unbelief, expounds the priestly office of Christ throughout this letter.

Indeed, what comfort can we have in God Himself
but through Christ? And what comfort can we have in
Christ Himself but as He is clothed in His priestly garments, in His office of High Priest? All the comfort we
have in the other offices of Christ—namely, His kingly
and His prophetic offices—is based on His priestly office.
His priesthood gives life, being, and efficacy to both other
offices. This is why the high priest in the Old Testament,
as a type of Christ, wore a crown upon his head and the
breastplate of Urim and Thummim upon his breast, thus
showing that both the kingly and prophetic offices were
planted upon the priestly office of Jesus Christ.

Indeed, if you look in the first three chapters of Revelation, you will find that all the other titles and attributes of God, which are streams of comfort flowing down upon the churches, all come from this fountain of Jesus Christ's priestly office. In Revelation 2:1, the Lord Christ used this title: "He who holds the seven stars in His right hand." Then, in Revelation 2:8, writing to the church of Smyrna, He took another title or attribute: "the First and the Last, who was dead, and came to life." In Revelation 2:12, writing to Pergamos, He took up another title: "He who has the sharp two-edged sword."

But now look at Revelation 1 and you will see that those various titles are summed up together in verse 16: "He had in His right hand seven stars" (His title to the church of Ephesus); "and out of His mouth went a sharp two-edged sword" (His title to the church of Pergamos); and in verses 17–18: "I am the First and the Last. I am He who lives, and was dead, and behold, I am alive forevermore" (His title to the church of Smyrna). But in verse 13, we see the fountain of all these streams: "and in the midst of the seven lampstands One like the Son of Man, clothed with a garment down to the feet and girded about the chest with a golden band."

This describes the robe and attire of the high priest, whose garment came down to his feet and was fastened with a golden girdle. So all these other attributes and titles of Christ originate here with Christ's priesthood, the fountainhead of all the other consolations.

The excellencies and attributes of Christ that are most beneficial to the saints are usually those that are most opposed by the world. And which title, attribute, or excellency of Christ is more opposed than His priestly office? What is anti-Christian religion, if not an opposition to Christ's priestly office? What is the popish Mass (that unbloody sacrifice), if not a denigration of Christ's singular sacrifice upon the cross and thus a denigration of His priestly office? What are penances and satisfactions, if not a denigration of Christ's ultimate satisfaction as our priest? And what are prayers to saints and angels, if not a denigration of Christ's priestly intercession? What does the pope call himself? The high priest—the very title that our Lord and Savior took for Himself. Thus, the whole body of popish doctrine is a great attack upon the priestly office of Jesus Christ.

Now the excellencies and attributes of Christ, which are usually most opposed by the world, are also those which bring the most comfort and benefit to God's people. And truly, the priestly office of Jesus Christ is an office of pure love and tender compassion, given in order to provide relief to poor, distressed sinners. Unlike His other offices, there is no mixture of terror in Christ's priestly office. As King, Christ rules over the church and all the world, but not everyone under His rule obtains mercy. "But bring here those enemies of mine, who did not want me to reign over them, and slay them before me" (Luke 19:27). Similarly, the prophetic office of Jesus

Christ extends to many who will never be saved. "And the light shines in the darkness, and the darkness did not comprehend it" (John 1:5). "He came to His own, and His own did not receive Him" (John 1:11). But wherever the priestly office of Jesus Christ is let forth upon a soul, that soul shall certainly be saved forever.

When faced with their sins, what great relief did the Jews have? They had many. When they were in the wilderness and stung by the fiery serpents, they had a brazen serpent to look upon as a relief against that distress. When they lacked water, they were given water out of a rock as a relief against that distress. When they lacked bread, they had manna from heaven as a relief against that distress. But when they sinned, where did they go? They took a sacrifice to the priest, and he would offer it for them. The priestly office, then, was the only relief they had against sin.

And so it is now—the priestly office of the Lord Jesus Christ is the only support and relief which Christians have against all temptations under heaven.

CHAPTER 2

Making Satisfaction

You might say to me, "Generalities do not affect me. Can you show in particular ways how the priestly office of Christ is the great storehouse of all our grace and comfort?"

To answer, I will begin with one particular aspect of the priestly office of Christ, showing how it is a relief and support against all temptations, a foundation of comfort, and a special means of grace and holiness.

Hebrews 2:17 says that the work of the high priest is "to make propitiation for the sins of the people." In the times of the Old Testament, the high priest made atonement for the people. When any man sinned, he brought a sacrifice, and his sins were laid upon the head of the sacrifice. Once every year the high priest entered into the Most Holy Place, and with the blood of the sacrifice, he sprinkled the mercy seat and laid the sins of the people upon the head of the scapegoat, thus making atonement for the people. This all appears clearly in Leviticus 16:14: "He shall take some of the blood of the bull and sprinkle it with his finger on the mercy seat on the east side; and before the mercy seat he shall sprinkle some of the blood with his finger seven times." Read also Leviticus 16:21: "Aaron shall lay both his hands on the head of the live goat, confess over it all the iniquities of the children of Israel, and all their transgressions, concerning all their sins, putting them on the head of the goat, and shall send it away into the wilderness by the hand of a suitable man." This was the work of the high priest: when the people had sinned, the high priest was to make atonement and satisfaction (which was just a type of Christ's satisfaction) for the sins of the people.

Now to better prove this great gospel truth I have presented, I shall insist on these five things:

1. When the Lord Jesus Christ died upon the cross, He offered up Himself as a sacrifice to God the Father.

2. The sins of all believers—past, present, and to come—were laid upon Jesus Christ.

3. When these sins were thus laid upon Christ, He thereby gave full satisfaction to God the Father and to divine justice.

4. Christ did all this as our Great High Priest and did so in a more transcendent and eminent manner than any high priest before Him.

5. This leads to our comfort and holiness.

Christ's Priestly Sacrifice

First, when the Lord Jesus Christ died upon the cross, He offered up Himself as a sacrifice to God the Father. Contrary to the Socinians, Christ did not die merely to give us an example for how to face death, but rather He offered up Himself as a sacrifice to God the Father. His sacrifice fulfilled everything to which all previous sacrifices pointed, and thus the things spoken of other sacrifices are also spoken of Him. For sacrifices may be either living sacrifices, or not, and of the inanimate sacrifices, they could be either solid (such as bread or grain) or liquid (such as wine or oil). But the thing offered was always destroyed. If a living thing was sacrificed, it was to be *slain*; and Jesus Christ is said to be "the Lamb slain from the foundation of the world" (Rev. 13:8). If bread or corn was offered, it was said to be *bruised*, and our Lord and Savior Christ "was bruised for our iniquities" (Isa. 53:5). If liquid, such as wine or oil, was offered, it was *poured out*, and so our Lord Savior "poured out His soul unto death" (Isa. 53:12). Thus, all sacrifices are fulfilled in Him.

When John the Baptist saw Christ he said, "Behold! The Lamb of God" (John 1:29). He did not say "behold the bull of God," or "behold the goat of God," even though bulls and goats were sacrificed. Why does he say "Lamb" instead of "bull" or "goat"? For when the high priest went into the Most Holy Place and sprinkled the mercy seat, he sprinkled it with the blood of a goat, not a lamb. Yet, notwithstanding, John said, "Behold! The Lamb of God." Why? The answer is not just because Christ was of a lamblike and meek disposition (as some say). Nor is the answer only because the great type of Christ was the paschal lamb (though this is true). Rather, in the temple there was a daily sacrifice, which was offered whether or not men brought any offerings. In the temple, this standing sacrifice was a lamb, not a goat. To show, therefore, that Jesus Christ is the daily sacrifice, John cried out, "Behold! The Lamb of God."

For proof, consider the apostle Paul's exhortation in Ephesians 5:2: "And walk in love, as Christ also has loved us and given Himself for us, an offering and a sacrifice to God for a sweet-smelling aroma." Here are three things to consider: First, he didn't say Christ "redeemed us," but that He "loved us." Second, Paul didn't say "who gave Himself for our sins," as he did in Galatians 1:4, but that He has "given Himself for us." Why? To show who they were that He gave Himself for—namely, sinners. Third, it says that He gave Himself as "an offering and a sacrifice"—not only an offering, but also as a sacrifice. This proves the first proposition: that our Lord Jesus, when He died on the cross, offered Himself as a sacrifice to God the Father.

He Bore Our Sins

Second, when this sacrifice was upon the altar, the sins of all believers—past, present, and to come—were laid upon Jesus Christ. Look at Isaiah 53:6:

All we like sheep have gone astray;
We have turned, every one, to his own way;
And the LORD has laid on Him the iniquity of
us all.

That which God lays on a person shall never be taken off by a person. And the Lord has laid on Jesus Christ the iniquities of us all.

Indeed, our iniquities are not only said to be laid on Him, but (to use the same word that is used for the sacrifice) it is said that He bore our sins on the cross. As the goat bore the sins of the people, Jesus "Himself bore our sins in His own body on the tree" (1 Peter 2:24).

Moreover, He did not only bear our sins upon the cross, but He was made "to be sin for us" (2 Cor. 5:21). It doesn't say that He was made a sinner or merely accounted as a sinner for us, but that He was made "to be sin for us." All our iniquities were laid on Him; He bore our sins; and He was made to be sin for us upon the cross. Thus the second proposition is proven, that when Christ offered up Himself upon the cross as a sacrifice, the sins of all believers were then laid upon Him.

God's Justice Satisfied

Third, when these sins were thus laid upon Christ, He thereby gave full satisfaction to God the Father and to divine justice. This is a foundation of much comfort. For if the Lord Jesus Christ, who is our surety, had not satisfied God the Father, who is the great creditor, to the utmost farthing for all our debts, then God the Father might come upon us, the debtors. But our surety, the Lord Christ, has given full satisfaction to God the Father, so that no more demands can be made upon us. And indeed, how else could Jesus have ever come out of prison? In the grave, He was under arrest, in jail. But the Father, the great creditor, let Him out. And not only this, but the Lord Jesus Christ went into heaven and sat down at the right hand of the Father. Surely, if the creditor had not been satisfied, the surety should never have been released from prison.

God the Father was so fully satisfied that He looked for iniquity and found none (Jer. 50:20). He looked over all His books to see if He could find anything in the record, but He found nothing—all our debts were paid.

Remember John the Baptist said, "Behold! The Lamb of God who takes away the sin of the world!" (John 1:29). John did not say "who takes away the sin of the Jews only," but he said, "who takes away the sin of the world." He did not say "who takes away the sins" (plural), but he said, "takes away the sin" (singular). For sins go together, as if they were but one. But let the sins be never so twisted together, as if it were but one sin, yet this Lamb of God takes away the sin of the world. And John did not say, "who has pardoned the sin of the world," for then a poor soul might say, "Yes, but though He has pardoned my sin, yet my sin is not mortified." And John did not say, "Behold the Lamb of God, who mortifies or destroys the sin of the world," but John gave us a word that takes in both pardon and mortification too. When John said, "Behold! The Lamb of God who takes away the sin of the world," it is as if John said, "Behold! The Lamb of God who takes sin away, both in regard to pardon and in regard to mortification."

Nothing so satisfies God the Father as obedience; and the fuller the obedience is, the more God the Father is satisfied by it. Now our Lord and Savior Christ, in this great sacrifice upon the cross, was obedient, for it is said He "became obedient to the point of death, even the death of the cross" (Phil. 2:8). What obedience, that He who made the law should come down from heaven to be subject to the law! Indeed, he was obedient to the point of deaths (plural), for Isaiah 53:9 says, "And they made His grave with the wicked—but with the rich at His death," and in this verse "death" is plural in the Hebrew, though it is singular in our English translation. It is as if, in some measure, the Holy Spirit had called the death that our Lord suffered "the second death" (Rev. 20:14). For if you truly and rightly consider things, I believe you will find that when our Lord and Savior Christ died and was in agony, He did not endure only the first death but also the torments of the second death. He could only conquer that which He first submitted Himself to, and He overcame death by submitting to death. But He overcame the second death as well, and therefore, in some measure, He submitted to its torments. What the first

Adam should have endured for his sin in the fall, Jesus endured as the second Adam in order to remove it. "In the day that you eat of it you shall surely die" (Gen. 2:17). This was not merely a bodily, outward death, but it was the second death. For if our Lord and Savior Christ did not endure the torments of the second death, the wrath of God upon His soul, why did He sweat drops of blood? Why did He so tremble and shake when He came to die? Many saints and martyrs go skipping, leaping, and rejoicing to death. But when our Lord and Savior came to die, He sweated drops of blood (Luke 22:44)! Surely there was more than an outward death. Oh, the wrath of God and the torments of the second death were upon His soul! Thus, He was obedient.

His obedience was voluntary, for He did not need to die for Himself, but He saw that God the Father was dishonored by human sin and that poor sinners would be lost. And rather than allow them to be lost, He voluntarily offered Himself to this obedience. Psalm 40:6–8 speaks of Jesus:

> Sacrifice and offering You did not desire;
> My ears You have opened.
> Burnt offering and sin offering You did not
>   require.
> Then I said, "Behold, I come;
> In the scroll of the book it is written of me.
> I delight to do Your will, O my God,
> And Your law is within my heart."

Mark what is said of Christ in this psalm, as it is plainly interpreted by the apostle in Hebrews 10:5–7:

> Sacrifice and offering You did not desire,
> But a body You have prepared for Me.
> In burnt offerings and sacrifices for sin
> You had no pleasure.
> Then I said, "Behold, I have come—
> In the volume of the book it is written of Me—
> To do Your will, O God."

The psalmist said, "My ears You have opened," or bored, as it is in Hebrew. The apostle translated these words as "a body You have prepared." Read them again as they are here in Psalm 40:6:

> Sacrifice and offering You did not desire;
> My ears You have opened [or bored].

Just as when a servant's ear was bored when he was willing to stay with his master and give him even more service, so the Lord Christ said: "I am as willing to do this work and to be thus obedient, as a servant whose ear has been bored is willing to stay with his master." Ah, here is obedience! And His obedience did so infinitely satisfy God the Father that Ephesians 5:2 says, "Christ also has loved us and given Himself for us, an offering and a sacrifice to God for a sweet-smelling aroma." Before, the whole world was full of a stench, and the Lord was displeased with mankind. But now that

Christ has come and offered up His sacrifice, He has given a full satisfaction to God the Father, and it is a sweet-smelling aroma, for the Father was fully satisfied.

To this I shall add one more word: when the Lord Jesus Christ offered up Himself as a sacrifice to God the Father, and our sins were laid upon Him, He gave a more perfect satisfaction to divine justice for our sins than if you and I and all of us had been damned in hell for all eternity. For a creditor is more satisfied when his debt is paid down all at once than if it is paid week by week. A poor man that cannot pay it all down at once will pay a small amount each week; but it is more satisfactory to the creditor to have it all paid at once. If all of us had been damned, we should have been but paying the debt a little at a time. But when Christ paid the debt, He paid it all down to God the Father. If we went to hell to be forever damned, God's justice would never be fully satisfied. But when Christ made satisfaction for our sins, God was satisfied.

Additionally, if the creditor is a merciful and a good man, he is more truly satisfied when the debtor is spared. He does not desire for the debtor to be cast into prison and there lie and rot. He is better satisfied by sparing the debtor. "Let me have but my money, and so the debtor be spared; I am willing, in fact, I desire it," says the good creditor. Now if we had all been cast into everlasting burnings, indeed, the debtor should have been paying the debt, but there the debtors would be lost. But instead Christ has come and made satisfaction to divine justice. Ah! The poor man is redeemed; the debtor is spared. Therefore, the Lord is infinitely more satisfied by the satisfaction that Christ made upon the cross for our sins than if we had all gone to hell and been damned for all eternity. Oh, what a glorious and blessed satisfaction our High Priest made to God the Father!

But you might then say, "If the Lord Christ made this full satisfaction to God the Father, how is it that many believers still have their sins and debts standing upon the score and are so perplexed in their consciences in regard to their sin, as if no satisfaction had been made?"

Luther called this aspect of sin a sacrilegious aspect and beholding of sin. He said it is as if a man took some goods from a holy place and brought them into his own house. This is sacrilege. So, Luther said, for me to take my sins from Christ and lay them upon my own heart is sacrilege.

The reason for this is because men do not study this truth and are ignorant of it. Suppose, for example, that a man owes three or four hundred pounds to a shopkeeper for wares and commodities that he has purchased, and a friend comes and pays the debt, crossing it out in the book. But when the debtor comes and looks upon the book, he is able to read all the particular purchases. Since he is not acquainted with the nature of the friend's crossing out the debt, he reads the list of particular purchases and charges it upon himself, and he is much troubled about how to pay the debt as if it were not paid at all. So it is for us—the Lord Jesus Christ has come and crossed out our sin in the book with His own blood. When the sins are read in our own consciences, when we are not acquainted with the nature of Christ's satisfaction and the crossing out of our sin, we charge ourselves, as if no sin had been satisfied for us. Yet when the Lord Jesus Christ made an offering for sin upon the cross, He gave a full satisfaction to God the Father.

The Highest High Priest

Fourth, Christ did all this as our Great High Priest, and He did so in a more transcendent and eminent manner than any high priest before Him. In the Old Testament, while the high priest made atonement for a poor sinner, he was not himself the sacrifice. But Christ as our Great High Priest not only offered a sacrifice, but He also offered Himself as the sacrifice. The sacrifice in the Old Testament could not purge the conscience, not only because it was the blood of bulls and goats (Heb. 9:12), but also because the sacrifice was performed successively. A man sinned, then brought a sacrifice; then he sinned again and had to bring another sacrifice. And once every year, the high priest went into the Most Holy Place to make atonement. But meanwhile, a poor soul might have thought, "What if I die before the yearly atonement comes about? What will become of me? The high priest goes once a year into the Most Holy Place and sprinkles blood on the mercy seat, but what will become of me if I die before that time?" But now, our Great High Priest has not only offered Himself up as the sacrifice, but has also offered up this sacrifice once for all (Heb. 9:12). So now, when a Christian has sinned, he is not to think of a sacrifice that is yet to come, but instead is to look to that which has already been accomplished: the sacrifice offered once for all. Therefore, the Christian does not need to live in suspense now, as did the Jews. The Christian's conscience can be fully purged from sin.

Again, take the high priest in the times of the Old Testament. Though he made atonement for the sins of the people, he also sometimes led the people into sin. Concerning the golden calf, it is said that Aaron, the great high priest, made the people naked (Ex. 32:25). But the Lord Jesus Christ, our Great High Priest, made atonement for sin and never leads us into sin. He is so far from making us naked, that He covers us with His righteousness that our nakedness may not appear. Here is a glorious High Priest.

Indeed, this High Priest of ours not only paid the past debt, but He became our surety for the time to come. None of the high priests in the Old Testament did this—Aaron and all the other high priests never guaranteed God the Father that a sinner would sin no more. But our Lord Jesus Christ, our High Priest, became our surety. And what kind of surety? Not an ordinary surety. For among us the surety cosigns with the debtor, but the debt continues in the debtor's name, so that he himself pays the debt. But Christ as our surety provides the guarantee and pays the debt for us. There is not a godly man or believer who ever guaranteed God the Father to pay the debt himself. But our surety came and made the guarantee in His own name, taking the debtor's name out.

Oh, what a glorious and blessed High Priest we have! Here is a High Priest, greater than all the high priests who ever came before!

Our Comfort and Holiness

Fifth, the satisfaction of Christ as our High Priest leads to our comfort and holiness.

Comfort

God has set up a storehouse of mercy and has erected an office of love out of mere compassion for poor sinners. God the Father has been satisfied, and our sins have been pardoned. Is this not comforting in the ears of a poor sinner? Christ said to the paralytic, "Son, your sins are forgiven you" (Mark 2:5). He did not say, "Your disease is healed." No, whether the disease is healed or not, this is comfort: "Son, your sins are forgiven you."

The believer can therefore say, "If the Lord Jesus Christ has made satisfaction for my sin, then whatever afflictions may come, they do not come as a punishment for my sins." When a reprobate is smitten and afflicted, all his miseries are as so many arrests for him to pay down his debt. But has the Lord Jesus Christ satisfied divine justice? Has he satisfied God the Father on a believer's behalf? Then surely these afflictions do not come as punishments so that a believer should make satisfaction for his or her sins.

Again, a believer may say, "If the Lord Jesus Christ has satisfied divine justice for my sins, then I shall never be damned and I shall never fall from grace. I have had many fears that I should fall from grace and so go to hell and perish at last, but if the Lord Jesus Christ has satisfied divine justice for my sin, then God the Father will never punish my sin again, for it was punished in Jesus Christ. Therefore, I cannot fall from grace, and therefore, I can never be damned."

If the Lord Jesus Christ has satisfied divine justice as our Great High Priest, then we may come with boldness to the throne of grace. As long as their debts are unpaid, debtors do not dare to come by the prison door. They are afraid of every sergeant and afraid of their friends that they might be sergeants. But when their debts are paid, then they dare to go about with boldness. And so, the poor souls, when they know that Christ has satisfied justice and that their debts are paid, then they may go with boldness to the throne of grace.

But you might say, "I cannot have this comfort because I cannot say that Christ has made satisfaction for me. How shall I know that Jesus Christ is my High Priest and has made satisfaction for me? Ah, if I did but know that the Lord Jesus Christ were my High Priest, then I would have comfort indeed. How can I know this? I am afraid He has not satisfied for me!"

But why not for you, man or woman? Why not for you? I shall tell you what I have heard concerning a young man who lay upon his deathbed and went to heaven. While he was lying upon his deathbed, he comforted himself that the Lord Christ had died for sinners. "Oh, blessed be the Lord," he said, "Jesus Christ has died for me!" But Satan came in with these words to tempt him: "Yes, but, young man, why for you? Christ died for sinners, but why for you? How can you know that Christ died for you?" The man said, "No, Satan. And why not for me? Ah! The Lord Jesus—He died for sinners, and therefore, Satan, why not for me?" So he held on to his comfort and went to heaven triumphing. So say I to you, poor drooping soul, laboring under temptation: "Why not for you? Why not for you?" And say you can say to Satan, "Why not for me?"

Again, Christ's satisfaction lies open for all sorts of sinners to come to it. The promise is made to all who will receive it. If someone comes to the promise and applies it, their very application of the promise makes it theirs. If you say, "Oh, if I could but know that the promise belongs to me," then I say that your very resting upon the promise makes it yours.

Furthermore, if Jesus Christ is willing for you to think that He has made satisfaction for you, then it is no presumption for you to think so. At the Lord's Supper, He said, "Take my blood that is shed for you; I apply it to you" (see Luke 22:20). And behold your King comes to you. When the prophet spoke of Jesus riding on a donkey, he did not say, "Behold, your King is coming," but said, "Behold, your King is coming *to you*" (Matt. 21:5).

Furthermore, if poor Christians cannot now go to Jesus Christ as their High Priest and say, "Jesus is a High Priest for me," then we are in a much worse condition than the Jews were. For when Jews had sinned, they could always carry their sacrifice to the high priest and say, "This is a high priest for me." Once the high priest had sprinkled blood on the mercy seat, any Jew in the Old Testament could say, "He did this for me." And we are not in a worse condition than they were, for our High Priest is beyond all the high priests who came before Him. Therefore, any poor Christian may go to the Lord Christ and say, "Oh, my High Priest has made satisfaction for me!" What a comfort this is to poor, drooping souls! Lift up your heads all you saints and children of God.

When there is no running water in a river, then a ship is grounded upon the sand, but when the tide comes in, the ship is raised and comes off the sand. And as long as you have nothing in your own channel but your own righteousness, you will be stuck in the sand, in the deep mire. But when the tide of the Lord's satisfaction comes in, there is a sea full of mercy that is able to lift the heaviest vessel. How this lifts up poor souls from the sand of their own righteousness! Be of good comfort.

Holiness

But you may say, "Does this also lead to our grace or holiness? And if so, then how?" Yes, this truth also leads to holiness. The new covenant of grace is founded upon Jesus Christ's offering and satisfaction upon the cross. The apostle mentioned the new covenant of grace three times in Hebrews, in chapters 8, 9, and 10. In all these places, he founded the covenant of grace on the satisfaction of Jesus Christ, but especially in Hebrews 9:13–15:

> For if the blood of bulls and goats and the ashes of a heifer, sprinkling the unclean, sanctifies for the purifying of the flesh, how much more shall the blood of Christ, who through the eternal Spirit offered Himself without spot to God, cleanse your conscience from dead works to serve the living God? And for this reason He is the Mediator of the new covenant, by means of death, for the redemption of the transgressions under the first covenant, that those who are called may receive the promise of the eternal inheritance.

Since the new covenant of grace is clearly built upon this part of Christ's priestly office, namely His satisfaction, you may now go to God the Father and say, "Lord, You have made a covenant of grace with poor sinners, and this covenant is founded on the priestly office and satisfaction of Jesus Christ. The Lord Jesus Christ has made satisfaction for me. And the new covenant promises that we 'shall all be taught of God' (John 6:45). Oh Lord, I am ignorant! Therefore, by Christ's satisfaction, teach me now that I may become wise for salvation. Lord, in the covenant of grace, you say, 'I will put My laws into their hearts' (Heb. 10:16). Now, Lord, seeing that Jesus Christ has founded this covenant in His blood and that I am one of those He has made satisfaction for, oh, write Your law in my heart that I may do all Your will."

We also see that this leads to our holiness because it strengthens our faith. If faith is weak, then all grace is weak, but if you strengthen your faith, then you strengthen your holiness, as well as all other graces. You don't strengthen the branch of a tree by carrying fertilizer up the tree to lay on the branch, but by spreading it at the root. If you strengthen the roots, you strengthen all the branches. Well, faith is the root grace. And knowing and thoroughly digesting the truth that the Lord Jesus Christ is our High Priest who has made satisfaction for us wonderfully strengthens our faith. For the more I know that God and Christ are willing to show mercy to me, the more my faith is strengthened.

We know that every person, if faithful, is willing to do the work that pertains to their office. Porters are willing to carry burdens. Why? Because it belongs to their office. It is their job. Similarly, bearing our sins belongs to the office of Jesus Christ as our High Priest.

Surely, therefore, He is willing to do it, for He is faithful in His office.

The more I see the holy necessity of Christ to show mercy to me, the more my faith rises. This is a very remarkable thing—the Lord Jesus Christ, as God, may refuse to show mercy, but as our High Priest, Jesus cannot and will not refuse the poor sinner who comes to Him. If I know that Christ is able to show mercy, my faith stirs a little at the sight of His ability. If I know that He is willing to show mercy to me, my faith rises higher. But if I know that Christ cannot refuse me when I come to Him, then my faith rises to a great height indeed!

When poor sinners among the Jews had sinned and brought their sacrifices to the high priest, the priest could not refuse them. And our Lord Jesus Christ as our Great High Priest cannot refuse us. As God, He may refuse, but being our High Priest, He cannot refuse a poor sinner who comes to Him for mercy. Oh, what a great strengthening this is to faith! And if you strengthen faith, you strengthen all other graces.

Furthermore, the more people are engaged to Jesus Christ and He takes them to be engaged to Him, the more holy they are. The more they see themselves as freed from sin by Christ, the more they take themselves to be engaged to Christ. If a person was about to be locked in debtor's prison for a great sum of money but someone came to the sergeant at the last minute and said, "Hold on—here is the money! I will pay this person's debt," wouldn't the poor debtor feel forever engaged to the friend who paid the debt and freed him or her from imprisonment? So it is with the Lord Christ. Ah, we were all going to prison—everlasting prison, chains of darkness—and He came and laid down the money. He made full satisfaction to God the Father as our Great High Priest. He paid our debt. Oh, how knowing this truth thus engages every soul to the Lord Christ, to become His forever!

Lastly, the more people deny their own righteousness, the more holy they are with gospel holiness. It is said that the Jews, by going about to establish their own righteousness, did not submit to the righteousness of Christ (Rom. 10:3). But in contrast, when people go about to establish the righteousness of Christ and submit to it, they then deny their own righteousness. The more we see the fullness of Jesus Christ's satisfaction to God the Father for all our sins, the more we acknowledge and establish Christ's righteousness and the more we shall stop depending on our own righteousness.

Oh, therefore, as ever you desire to have more grace, more holiness, and more comfort, study—and study much—this priestly office of Jesus Christ! Many people complain that they cannot profit under the means of grace: that they have hard hearts, that the ways and ordinances of God are not sweet to them. They perform prayers but with no sweetness. They don't relish the blood and Spirit of Christ upon their hearts in their duties. They complain that their sins and temptations are too mighty for them, and that one day they shall be slain by the hands of some lust or corruption. No wonder we have these complaints when we don't go to the storehouse of comfort and grace that the Lord has opened for us. The priestly office of Christ is the great storehouse of all the grace and comfort we have this side of heaven. If you don't go to it, is there any wonder that you lack comfort or grace?

I appeal to you now, are there not this day some— no, many—who have never gone to Jesus Christ as their High Priest? Are there not even some who have publicly professed faith who do not understand the priestly office of Jesus Christ? No wonder, poor soul, that you are so uncomfortable and have no more strength against your temptations.

Suppose the state should appoint a man to relieve poor, maimed soldiers who are begging. If they met with the same man in the streets and begged of him as an ordinary citizen, he may not relieve them. But if they come to him, as a man appointed by the State for their relief, then he relieves them according to his office and duty. So it is sometimes with men and women: they might go to Christ in an ordinary way, but not as the great Lord Treasurer of all our graces, as our Great High Priest. They do not go to Him according to His office, as established by God the Father for the relief of sinners, and they do not address themselves to Him as their High Priest who will make satisfaction for them. Therefore, they go away without relief.

Do we want more strength against corruption? Do we want to walk with more comfort? Do we want to find the ways of God, the ordinances and duties, sweeter and more comforting to our souls? Then read and consider that verse in Song of Songs 2:3:

> Like an apple tree among the trees of the woods,
> So is my beloved among the sons.
> I sat down in his shade with great delight,
> And his fruit was sweet to my taste.

The spouse this verse is speaking of is Christ. What is this fruit of Christ? Your justification, adoption, calling, sanctification, and consolation—it is all the fruit of Christ. And all your own duties, your prayers, reading, meditation, they are all the fruit of Christ. The enjoyment of all his ordinances and all your spiritual privileges under the gospel are the fruit of Christ. The spouse said,

> I sat down in his shade with great delight,
> And his fruit was sweet to my taste.

Someone who loves fruit, such as pears, apples, or cherries, might say, "I love this fruit, but I need to go where this fruit grows to gather it off the tree because I don't have any fruit in my house." So it is with the bride of Jesus Christ. Perhaps we have sought fruit in the shade of other trees. Perhaps we have sat down in the shade of our possessions, our friendships, or something else and have enjoyed that fruit. Well, behold here a tree, the tree of life, whose shade reaches to the ends of the earth. Come and sit down in its shade!

If you have never known true comfort, come sit in the shade of the Lord Jesus Christ's priestly office and enjoy its fruit. Come, you who say you cannot profit under the means of grace; come, you who complain of various temptations and sins; come, you whose consciences have never known comfort or peace. Come now and sit under this tree. I tell you, from the Lord, that this fruit will be sweet to your taste. You will go to prayer and find it sweet to your soul, though up till now you have found no sweetness in it. The word and other ordinances will be sweeter to you "than honey and the honeycomb" (Ps. 19:10).

Thus, it is evident how the priestly office of Jesus Christ brings us comfort and leads us to holiness. Oh, let us therefore study the priestly office of Jesus Christ and come sit down in His shade, and the Lord will make His fruit sweet to our souls!

CHAPTER 3

Making Intercession

We have seen that the priestly office of Jesus Christ is the great storehouse of all the grace and comfort which we have in this world and that by this we obtain comfort and relief against all temptations. We have seen that this is generally true, and we have demonstrated this in one aspect of the high priest's work, the making of satisfaction for sin.

By looking further into the work of the high priest, to find more help in addressing ourselves to Jesus Christ, we learn that the high priest's work was also to intercede or pray for the people. As Hebrews 2:17 says, His work was "to make propitiation for the sins of the people."

In the Old Testament, this propitiation, or atonement, was made not only by offering a sacrifice but by taking its blood and presenting it with prayers and intercessions to God. We see this in Leviticus 16. After the sacrifice was killed, the priest was to take the blood and sprinkle it on the mercy seat (v. 14). In verses 12 and 13, we read, "Then he shall take a censer full of burning coals of fire from the altar before the LORD, with his hands full of sweet incense beaten fine, and bring it inside the veil. And he shall put the incense on the fire before the LORD, that the cloud of incense may cover the mercy seat that is on the Testimony, lest he die." Thus, the priest was to cause a cloud of incense to arise upon the mercy seat.

All this was a type of the prayers and intercessions of Jesus Christ, who, having offered up Himself once and for all as a sacrifice for our sins, has carried the virtue of His blood into heaven and there sprinkles the mercy seat and intercedes for us. As we read in Hebrews 9:11–12, "But Christ came as High Priest of the good things to come, with the greater and more perfect tabernacle not made with hands, that is, not of this creation. Not with the blood of goats and calves, but with His own blood He entered the Most Holy Place once for all, having obtained eternal redemption." And in verse 24, "For Christ has not entered the holy places made with hands, which are copies of the true, but into heaven itself, now to appear in the presence of God for us."

When you give due consideration to this in Hebrews, you will find that Christ's intercession is the essential work of His priestly office. His intercession doesn't fall short of His satisfaction, but rather goes beyond it. "For if He were on earth, He would not be a priest" (Heb. 8:4). For in the Old Testament, if the priest had only offered a sacrifice but had not gone into the Most Holy Place to sprinkle its blood on the mercy seat and to pray that it might be accepted for the sins of the people, then the priest would not have completed his priestly work. So now, if Jesus Christ had only offered Himself as a sacrifice, but had not carried the virtue and power of His death into heaven to pray and intercede for us there, then His priestly work would be incomplete. In the Old Testament, though every priest could sacrifice, only the high priest could go into the Most Holy Place. So, therefore, Jesus Christ's intercession for us in heaven is His great and special work as our High Priest.

In order to clarify this mysterious truth, I shall expound it by showing four things:

1. the nature and work of Christ's intercession;

2. the prevailing power of Christ's intercession with God the Father;

3. the transcendent superiority of Christ's intercession as our High Priest above all those who went before; and

4. how this leads to our comfort and holiness.

What Intercession Means

What is the nature of Christ's intercession? In what does it consist? First, it consists in this: He appeared for us in heaven, owning our cause and our souls to God the Father. This is seen in Hebrews 9:24: "For Christ has not entered the holy places made with hands, which are copies of the true, but into heaven itself, now to appear in the presence of God for us." He did not appear for us in heaven in an ordinary manner, but rather with an emphasis—He appears openly and publicly, before all the saints and angels, in the presence of God the Father. It often encourages someone to have a good friend in court to appear on his behalf. But when there is any danger, this good friend might not appear and own this other person as a friend. But we have a friend in heaven who appears for us and owns our cause and our souls in all conditions.

Second, He not only appears for us, but by virtue of His priestly office, He carries the power, merit, and virtue of His blood into the presence of God the Father in heaven and sprinkles the mercy seat with it seven times. The number seven notes perfection. Christ intercedes for those for whom He has suffered. He takes their debts, carries them to God the Father, and says, "Father, I have paid these debts. I have satisfied Your justice for these poor sinners. Now, I ask for them to be pardoned and acquitted" (see Heb. 9:11–12).

Third, he not only carries the power and virtue of His blood, presenting it to God the Father for our discharge, but He also pleads our cause in heaven, answering all the accusations brought against us. As the apostle says in Romans 8:33–34: "Who shall bring a charge against God's elect? It is God who justifies. Who is he who condemns? It is Christ who died, and furthermore is also risen, who is even at the right hand of God, who also makes intercession for us." Notice the basis of how the apostle speaks: Who shall condemn them? Jesus Christ is at the right hand of God the Father to take away the accusations brought against them. Let the world condemn, let Moses condemn, let Satan condemn; Jesus Christ is at the Father's right hand to take away all these accusations.

There is a clear and full illustration of this in Zechariah 3. Satan is standing at Joshua's right hand to oppose him: "Then he showed me Joshua the high priest standing before the Angel of the LORD, and Satan standing at his right hand to oppose him" (v. 1). It was the accuser's custom to stand at the right hand of the accused (see Ps. 109:6). And here Satan stands at Joshua's right hand, noting his accusations against him. What did he accuse him of? Look at verse 3: "Now Joshua was clothed with filthy garments, and was standing before the Angel." Satan came and accused Joshua of his filthy garments. And, indeed, he did have filthy garments, for the priests had defiled themselves in Babylon by marrying strange wives, as Joshua and his children are so charged in Ezra 10:18.

In other words, there was substance in Satan's accusation, for Joshua had defiled his garments. But now our Lord Jesus Christ, our Great High Priest, stepped in and took away the accusation, saying to Satan, "The LORD rebuke you, Satan! The LORD who has chosen

Jerusalem rebuke you! Is this not a brand plucked from
the fire?" (Zech. 3:2). The Septuagint uses the same
word that is used for excommunication, which is here
repeated twice: "The LORD rebuke you!... The LORD...
rebuke you." This shows not only the fullness of Satan's
rebuke, but the fullness of Jesus Christ's intercession.

It is as if he said, "It is true, Lord, that Joshua has
filthy garments. Nevertheless, Joshua is but a newly
plucked brand from the burning fire. When you first
pull a brand from the fire, there will be dust, ashes, and
dirt. But, although Joshua has dust, ashes, and dirt—
although he is clothed with filthy garments—I will take
them away." So, in verse 4, "Then He answered and spoke
to those who stood before Him, saying, 'Take away the
filthy garments from him.' And to him He said, 'See, I
have removed your iniquity from you, and I will clothe
you with rich robes.'" This can be speaking of none
but Christ.

Thus Christ took away the accusation brought
against Joshua by Satan, for his filthy garments. And
so does the Lord Christ for us now. If a poor soul falls
into any sin and defiles his garments, Satan comes in
and stands at his right hand and accuses, by reason of
his filthy garments. But our Lord Jesus Christ, our Great
High Priest, who is at the right hand of the Father, takes
up our cause and answers the accusation: "True, Lord,
this poor soul, indeed, has filthy garments, but he is like a
firebrand newly plucked out from the fire. He was in his

sinful condition. He was burning. But now he is changed, and though he still has filth upon him, I will take away his filthy garments and clothe him in rich robes." So it is that the Lord Christ steps in to God the Father and answers all the accusations brought against us.

Again, He not only pleads our cause and takes away the accusations brought against us but He also calls for God the Father's absolution and pardon of poor sinners. He does this with justice and equity. That is why He is called our Advocate. "And if anyone sins, we have an Advocate with the Father, Jesus Christ the righteous" (1 John 2:1). The work of an advocate differs from the work of a petitioner. An advocate does not merely petition the judge, but an advocate tells the judge what is right according to the law. So the Lord Jesus Christ, who is making intercession for us in heaven, is there as our Advocate. "Lord," He says, "these people have indeed sinned. But I have made satisfaction for their sins. I have fully paid for them. I have satisfied your wrath to the full. Now, therefore, in justice and equity, I call for their pardon." Thus, Christ intercedes, and we see, briefly, the nature and work of His intercession.

Christ's Prevailing Prayers

Suppose Jesus does intercede—can He prevail in His intercession? Do His prayers have power with God the Father? Yes, very much. We find in Zechariah 3 that Joshua goes away with a clean turban upon his head:

And I said, "Let them put a clean turban on his head."

So they put a clean turban on his head, and they put the clothes on him. And the Angel of the LORD stood by. (v. 5)

At the beginning, Satan stood at Joshua's right hand to accuse him. But the accuser of the brethren went away with a double rebuke, and Joshua, through the intercession of Jesus Christ, went away with a crown upon his head.

The prevailing power of Christ's intercession is clear when we consider three things.

First, consider what great interest our Lord and Savior Christ has in the bosom of God the Father. Paul prevailed with Philemon for Onesimus through the great interest that Paul had in the heart of Philemon. Our Lord and Savior Christ is in the bosom of God the Father for all eternity (John 1:18). He is the Father's Son: His natural Son, His beloved Son, His Son who never offended Him; surely, therefore, the Son will prevail when He comes and intercedes for a man or woman.

We know that when David went out against Nabal and his house, Abigail came to meet David and intercede for Nabal. She so powerfully interceded for Nabal that she turned David's heart. David had sworn he would not leave one male of Nabal's house, but after Abigail interceded, David said to Abigail, "Blessed is the LORD God of Israel, who sent you this day to meet me! And blessed is your advice and blessed are you, because you have kept me this day from coming to bloodshed and from avenging myself with my own hand" (1 Sam. 25:32–33). What did she say that turned David? She said that, true to his name, Nabal was a foolish man and she urged David to spare him so that it would not later be a grief to his heart (vv. 25–31), and thus she prevailed with David. Abigail was a stranger to David, and she prayed for a wicked, vile, and foolish man; shall not the Lord Jesus Christ, the Father's Son, who is not a stranger to the Father, but His beloved from everlasting, shall He not prevail much more when He pleads the cause of the elect children of God in the presence of His Father?

Great is a child's rhetoric when crying "Father." If children are wise, they can prevail much with a tenderhearted father. The Lord Jesus Christ is the Son of the Father and the wisdom of the Father too. And God the Father is a tenderhearted Father. Surely, then, Jesus Christ's intercession with God the Father is powerful.

Second, we see the power of Christ's intercession when we consider how the Father is inclined and disposed to grant the same things for which Christ prays. If children should entreat their father in a matter the father has no inclination to grant or is set against, then the children might not prevail. But if beloved children ask the father for something the father also likes, they are likely to succeed. When the Lord Jesus Christ intercedes for us, the Father has as great an inclination and disposition toward

the work Christ intercedes for, just as Christ Himself has.
That is why Christ said, "Behold, I have come to do Your
will. I came not to do My own will, but the will of Him
who sent Me" (see John 6:38; Heb. 10:7). The Father is
as strongly inclined and disposed to what Christ did and
wills as Christ Himself. He also said, "Of those You have
given Me, I have lost none. They are Yours, and therefore,
I pray for them" (see John 17:6–12).

Look at a notable example in John 10:17. Jesus said,
"Therefore My Father loves Me, because I lay down My
life that I may take it again." He said, "I lay down My
life," referring to His suffering and satisfaction, and "that
I may take it again," referring to His going up to heaven
and interceding. But what else did He say? "Therefore
My Father loves Me." Oh, what a round of love is here!
God the Father out of love sent Christ into the world to
die for men and women: "For God so loved the world
that He gave His only begotten Son" (John 3:16). Jesus
Christ, out of love for us, died for us: "Christ…has loved
us and given Himself for us" (Eph. 5:2). The Father
loved the world by giving Christ. The Son loved the
world by dying for us. And the Father loves Christ again
for loving us. Christ loves us, and the Father loves Christ
again for loving us. What a wonderful expression—
that the Father should love Christ for loving us!

Consider then that the Father's inclination and disposition toward the love of Christ shown to poor sinners
is just as strong as Christ's. So, when He comes to God

the Father to intercede, He will prevail because the Father loves Him for interceding. The Father loves Christ's work as much as Christ does; He loves Him even more for it.

Third, we see the power of Christ's intercession when we consider the terms upon which our Great High Priest was taken and admitted into heaven, the Most Holy Place. Christ was received into heaven with honor. And He was received there that He might fulfill His work as the High Priest. He was honorably received into heaven, and He was received there to do the work of the High Priest. The Father said to Him, "Sit at My right hand" (Heb. 1:13)—a place of honor. When Solomon wanted to express his honor to his mother, he had her sit at his right hand (1 Kings 2:19), just as God the Father expressed the honorable welcome of Christ into heaven.

Now observe that whenever sitting at the right hand of the Father was mentioned, it did not concern Christ's kingly office but His priestly office. You would expect it to refer to His kingly office, but you will find, running through the Scriptures, that sitting at the right hand is connected to His priestly office. Look at Hebrews 8:1: "Now this is the main point of the things we are saying: We have such a High Priest, who is seated at the right hand of the throne of the Majesty in the heavens." We see it again in Hebrews 10:11–12: "And every priest stands ministering daily and offering repeatedly the same sacrifices, which can never take away sins. But this Man, after He had offered one sacrifice for sins forever, sat down at the right hand of God." His session is carried along with the mention of His priestly office, as if He sat down at the Father's right hand in heaven in order to fulfill His work as the High Priest.

Thus, when Jesus Christ came into heaven, into the Most Holy Place, He came there as our Great High Priest. And He said to God the Father, "Lord, I have not come in My own name, for My own sake only, but I have come as the Great High Priest, having on this breastplate the names of all the elect. And as High Priest, I come to intercede for poor sinners." And God the Father said to Him, "Welcome upon those terms. Though You come in their names, come sit down at My right hand." We see then how the Father is engaged to hear the intercession of Jesus Christ, for He received Christ into heaven upon those terms as our Great High Priest. Therefore, the intercession of Jesus Christ has great and prevailing power with God the Father in heaven.

Christ's Superior Intercession

Consider the transcendent superiority of Christ's intercession as our High Priest above all those who went before Him. Does the Lord Jesus Christ intercede for us in heaven as our Great High Priest? Yes, and He does this in a more transcendent and eminent way and manner than any high priest before Him.

We know this, first, because He has gone through more temptations than any high priest before Him. "For in that He Himself has suffered, being tempted, He is able to aid those who are tempted" (Heb. 2:18). And He was tempted as our High Priest. If He was tempted that He might help those who are tempted, and help them as their High Priest, then the more He was tempted, the more He is experientially able to help those who are tempted.

There was never a high priest who was tempted like Christ. He "was in all points tempted as we are, yet without sin" (Heb. 4:15). Poor soul, name any temptation that frightens your heart, and you will find the Lord Jesus Christ was tempted with that temptation. You might say, "I am often tempted to doubt whether I am the child of God." So was Christ. You know the place where the devil tempted Him, saying, "If You are the Son of God..." (Matt. 4:3, 6). Two times, the devil set an "if" upon Christ's sonship. Or perhaps you say, "Oh, but I am often tempted to use indirect means to get out of trouble!" So was Christ. The devil said to Him, "Command that these stones become bread" (v. 3). Or perhaps you say, "Oh, but sometimes I have even been tempted to lay violent hands upon myself!" The devil tempted Christ in this way too, when he tempted Him to throw Himself down from the pinnacle of the temple (v. 5). Or perhaps you say, "Oh, but I am tempted to such evil things that truly I am afraid to speak of them—such blasphemies, such horrid, wretched blasphemies that I think have never come upon the heart of any child of God, so I am afraid to think of them and ashamed to mention them!" Yet was not Christ likewise tempted? The devil said to Him, "All these things I will give You if You will fall down and worship me" (v. 9). Oh, horrid blasphemy! Blush, blush, oh, sun, that the Lord Jesus, the God of glory, should fall down and worship the devil! What wretched blasphemy was here, that the devil should speak this! And yet the Lord Jesus Christ was tempted to it.

What shall I say? He was in all things tempted as we are, yet without sin. No previous high priest had ever been tempted like this. But Christ was thus tempted in order to help those who are tempted. He is more able as our High Priest to intercede—to put in for you and to help you—than any high priest ever was before Him.

Again, just as He has gone through more tempta-tions than any previous high priest, so He is also filled with more compassion. It was fitting for the high priest to be merciful; it is an office of love and mercy. Now our Lord and Savior Christ is such a High Priest that He cannot help but be touched with your weaknesses. Those high priests who came before Him were sometimes not touched with people's weaknesses. Hannah came and prayed, and Eli's heart was not at first touched with her weakness. But our High Priest cannot help but be touched. He sympathizes with us in our weaknesses. He is afflicted in all our afflictions. Though it was the work of the high priest to sympathize with the people, there was a law that the high priest was not to mourn for his kindred so that he would not mourn as others. But now, our Lord Jesus fully sympathizes with us, and therefore He goes beyond all the high priests who were before Him.

Further, He is more faithful in His office than any high priest before Him. Aaron was a high priest, but he was unfaithful in the matter of the golden calf. But our Lord and Savior Christ is more faithful than Moses was. As we read in Hebrews 3:1–2, "Therefore, holy brethren, partakers of the heavenly calling, consider the Apostle and High Priest of our confession, Christ Jesus, who was faithful to Him who appointed Him, as Moses also was faithful in all His house." The author of Hebrews steps over Aaron the high priest and compares Christ to Moses in faithfulness. Now Moses was faithful in all His house, but our Lord and Savior is preferred before Moses in the point of faithfulness. Yet it is said: "Moses also was faithful in all His house." When the Lord commanded Moses anything, Moses did it. He was faithful, yet our Lord and Savior was more faithful than Moses. See verse 3: "For this One has been counted worthy of more glory than Moses, inasmuch as He who built the house has more honor than the house." And verses 5–6: "And Moses indeed was faithful in all His house as a servant, for a testimony of those things which would be spoken afterward, but Christ as a Son over His own house, whose house we are if we hold fast the confidence and the rejoicing of the hope firm to the end."

Look now: as a son is more faithful in his father's house than a servant will be, so Christ is more faithful than Moses. And as the builder of the house is superior to every beam and stone in the house, indeed every part of the building, so also Christ the Lord exceeds Moses in faithfulness. As there is a great difference between a stone in the building and the builder himself, so there is a great difference between Moses and Christ. Yet notwithstanding, Moses was faithful in all His house. Oh, then how faithful is Jesus Christ in His priesthood! In the matter of His priesthood, He is superior to all who came before.

Again, consider other high priests—no matter how good they were, they could not always intercede, for they would die. The high priest would die, and another would take his place. But Christ "always lives to make intercession" for us (Heb. 7:25).

Yes, take the high priest in the times of the Old Testament. Even while he lived, he did not always intercede for the people. Once a year, the high priest entered into the Most Holy Place to sprinkle the mercy seat with blood and cause a cloud to rise upon the mercy seat with his prayers and intercessions for their acceptance. Then he left the Most Holy Place and laid aside his garments. But now, our Great High Priest has ascended into the Most Holy Place, never to take off His priestly garments. And He doesn't sprinkle the mercy seat with

His sacrifice once a year, but every day. He is therefore superior to all the high priests who came before.

Furthermore, though the high priests in the Old Testament offered sacrifices and interceded for some sins, there were other sins for which no sacrifice could be offered. If a man accidentally killed someone, a sacrifice would be made. If a man sinned ignorantly, a sacrifice was made. But in Numbers 15:30 we read, "But the person who does anything presumptuously, whether he is native-born or a stranger, that one brings reproach on the LORD, and he shall be cut off from among his people." For this person, there was no sacrifice and no intercession.

But we have a High Priest who makes intercessions for all sins. So He Himself said, "All sins will be forgiven the sons of men, and whatever blasphemies they may utter; but he who blasphemes against the Holy Spirit never has forgiveness" (Mark 3:28–29). Every sin, though it boils up to blasphemy, will be forgiven— but there is no forgiveness without sacrifice. Therefore, Christ has made a sacrifice and thus presents the sacrifice and intercedes for poor sinners.

Our Comfort and Holiness
Comfort
First, this greatly leads to our comfort. Consider the "good and comforting words" spoken in Zechariah:

I saw by night, and behold, a man riding on a red horse, and it stood among the myrtle trees in the hollow; and behind him *were* horses: red, sorrel, and white. Then I said, "My lord, what are these?" So the angel who talked with me said to me, "I will show you what they are."

And the man who stood among the myrtle trees answered and said, "These are the ones whom the LORD has sent to walk to and fro throughout the earth."

So they answered the Angel of the LORD, who stood among the myrtle trees, and said, "We have walked to and fro throughout the earth, and behold, all the earth is resting quietly."

Then the Angel of the LORD answered and said, "O LORD of hosts, how long will You not have mercy on Jerusalem and on the cities of Judah, against which You were angry these seventy years?"

And the LORD answered the angel who talked to me, with good and comforting words." (1:8–13)

Let me explain this passage to show how the intercession of Jesus Christ leads to our comfort. In verse 8, the prophet sees a man riding on a red horse. This is the Lord Jesus Christ represented to us. He is called both a man (v. 8) and the Angel of the LORD (v. 11). And just as He walked among the golden candlesticks in the book of Revelation, here He stood among the saints and people of God, who were called myrtle trees for their greenness, sweetness, and fruitfulness. The myrtle trees were in the hollow to show how God's people are often in a dark, low, and poor condition. Behind Him were red, sorrel, and white horses, which represent the angels who are sent to and fro through the earth (vv. 9–10). Then, in verse 12, the Angel of the Lord interceded, saying, "O LORD of hosts, how long will You not have mercy on Jerusalem and on the cities of Judah, against which You were angry these seventy years?" This must be Christ, for no angel intercedes, but Christ alone. And what was the fruit of His intercession? "And the LORD answered the angel who talked to me, with good and comforting words" (v. 13). Yes, indeed! Good and comforting words are the fruit of Jesus Christ's intercession.

It is a matter of great comfort that the Lord Christ, our Great High Priest, is in heaven to intercede for us. Isn't it a comfort for a poor person to have a friend near the king or in court who is able to do him kindness? Sometimes a person might say, "I once had a true friend in court, but now he is dead." Yes, but here is a friend who never dies. He always lives to make intercession. Friends may change and even turn into enemies, but our Lord and Savior changes not. He said to His disciples, "Nevertheless do not rejoice in this, that the spirits are subject to you, but rather rejoice because your names are written in heaven" (Luke 10:20). It is a matter of great joy to have one's name written in heaven. Oh, but what is it then to have one's name written in the chief part of heaven! To have one's name written upon the breast-plate of Jesus Christ, our Great High Priest, who has gone into the Most Holy Place? And so it is—the Lord Christ has gone to heaven and entered the Most Holy Place and carries our names into the presence of God the Father, and there He pleads and intercedes for us. Oh, what comfort is here!

But you might say, "This is very good and comforting in itself. But what is this to me? For I am afraid the Lord does not intercede for me. If I could indeed persuade myself that the Lord Jesus were in heaven as *my* High Priest, to intercede for *me*, I truly think I would have comfort, though I were in the lowest condition, even in hell itself. But oh—I am afraid to bear myself upon the intercession of Jesus Christ, lest I should presume!

This is the great objection that continually stands in resistance to the comfort of God's people. Let me therefore fully deal with this objection and remove it so that this comfort may be fully yours. First, I will show it is no presumption for us to bear ourselves upon the intercession of Jesus Christ. Second, I will show those for whom the Lord Christ intercedes in heaven. And, third, I will show how infinitely willing He is to intercede for us so that I may bring comfort nearer to our own hearts.

First, it is not presumptuous for us to bear ourselves upon the intercession of Jesus Christ. It is not presumption to believe. We know the story of the woman who came to our Lord and Savior, who was cured by touching the hem of His garment. Our Savior, "immediately knowing in Himself that power had gone out of Him, turned around in the crowd and said, 'Who touched My clothes?'" (Mark 5:30). Then the woman came and fell down before Him, fearing and trembling. Our Lord and Savior Christ did not say to this poor woman, "How dare you touch Me? Why did you presume to touch Me?" But consider that the woman had no command to touch His garment for healing. She had no precept to back her and no promise that she would be healed by touching His garment. She had no example, for before this, no one had ever been healed by touching. No commandment, no promise, and no example. Surely now, if anyone was ever guilty of presuming, it was this woman, who had no commandment, no promise, and no example. Yet the Lord Jesus Christ did not chide her way. He did not tell her she had presumed, but He said, "Daughter, your faith has made you well. Go in peace, and be healed of your affliction" (Mark 5:34).

Allow me to drive this home. We have a command to believe in Christ. We have a promise that He always lives to make intercession for those who come to God through Him. And we have examples of many who have come to Jesus Christ and have entrusted themselves to His intercession and have gone away cured. What! It was not presumptuous for the woman to come and touch Christ without a commandment, a promise, or an example. So why would you say it is presumptuous for you to trust

Him when you have examples, promises, and command-
ments to believe? Be not deceived, it is not presumptuous
for you, poor soul, to bear yourself upon Jesus Christ.

Second, to bring this out more fully, I will show
those for whom the Lord Christ intercedes in heaven. "If
anyone sins, we have an Advocate with the Father, Jesus
Christ the righteous" (1 John 2:1). You might say, "This
is to be applied to those who were previously spoken
of, those who had fellowship with the Father." But read
this verse: "Truly our fellowship is with the Father and
with His Son Jesus Christ" (1 John 1:3). In other words,
if anyone who sins has fellowship with the Father or
with Christ, then they have an Advocate with God the
Father. Stand by, therefore. We grant that the comfort
of this doctrine of Christ's intercession belongs to anyone who has ever had fellowship with God the Father.

Moreover, in John 17 our Savior said that He prays
for those who do believe and those who will believe.
And it is these whom He intercedes for in heaven. He
said, "I do not pray for these alone, but also for those
who will believe in Me through their word" (v. 20). Well
then, here is another class of people—those who believe
and those who wait upon the Lord in the ordinance of
His word, that they may or shall believe. Therefore, you
shall stand by as well, for you are another class of people
to whom the comfort of Christ's intercession belongs.

Furthermore, if we look at Hebrews 7:25, we find
these words: "Therefore He is also able to save to the

uttermost those who come to God through Him, since He always lives to make intercession for them." And to whom is this referring? "Those who come to God through Him." Compare this with Isaiah 53:12, which clearly speaks of Christ:

> And He was numbered with the transgressors,
> And He bore the sin of many,
> And made intercession for the transgressors.

Maybe you cannot say, "I have fellowship with God the Father." And maybe you cannot say, "I believe. I am persuaded that I believe." Well, then, you can say this: "Through the Lord's grace I am coming to God through Christ. I have been and am a great transgressor, but I am coming to God through Christ. I am one of the coming transgressors. I have been a transgressor, but I am a coming transgressor; I come to God through Christ." You also, stand by. The intercession of the Lord Jesus Christ belongs to you too. For your comfort, let me tell you, poor soul, that no matter what you have been, you who now come to the Lord Jesus Christ, our Great High Priest, He has gone to heaven to intercede for your soul.

But you might say, "There is one thing that makes me afraid that He will not intercede for me. I have been so great a transgressor. Oh, I have sinned against this Great High Priest, and therefore I am afraid He will not intercede for me!"

For an answer, I only ask you to carefully consider Numbers 16:41–50. We read there that all the congregation murmured against Moses and Aaron. Aaron was the high priest, and the verse says, "All the congregation of the children of Israel complained against Moses and Aaron, saying, 'You have killed the people of the LORD.'" So, they murmured against Moses and Aaron. Then verse 46 says, "So Moses said to Aaron, 'Take a censer and put fire in it from the altar, put incense on it, and take it quickly to the congregation and make atonement for them; for wrath has gone out from the LORD. The plague has begun.'" Now notice what Aaron did: "Then Aaron took it as Moses commanded, and ran into the midst of the assembly; and already the plague had begun among the people. So he put in the incense and made atonement for the people. And he stood between the dead and the living; so the plague was stopped" (vv. 47–48). They had sinned against Aaron the high priest; nevertheless, he (who was but a type of Christ) stood between the dead and the living and made atonement for them. Oh, if there was such great compassion in Aaron, a type of Christ, that he would go intercede for them when they had sinned against him, how much more compassion to intercede for poor souls is there in our Lord Jesus Christ, the typified High Priest!

Third, to bring comfort more fully to our hearts, I will show how infinitely willing He is to intercede for us. We have seen that the intercession of Christ belongs to those who have had fellowship with the Father and with Christ, to those who do or shall believe, and to all those poor transgressors who come to God the Father through Christ. Now observe how infinitely willing the Lord Jesus Christ is to intercede for all such people.

For He is certainly willing to do that for which He received His anointing. It is said that Aaron was anointed and that the ointment ran down upon his beard and to the skirts of his garment. His entire garment was perfumed with this ointment. And surely the entire garment of Jesus Christ was also perfumed by His anointing. He is the Messiah, the Anointed One (Isa. 61:1). He was anointed with the oil of gladness above all His fellows (Ps. 45:7; Heb. 1:9), above all the high priests who came before. And He was anointed for this very purpose: to do the work of the high priest, which is to intercede for the sins of the people. Therefore 1 John 2:1 says, "If anyone sins, we have an Advocate with the Father, Jesus Christ." Who is this Advocate? He is Jesus, your Savior, and He is willing to intercede. Perhaps you might say, "Yes, but what if He is not able to intercede? Maybe he hasn't received the anointing to do it." Ah, but He is also called Christ, and the name Christ signifies Anointed One. He is therefore anointed for this very purpose—to be your Advocate.

Now if a man receives money to use for the benefit of others, such as poor orphans, then if he is faithful, he will certainly use the money for them, in accord with the purpose of whoever entrusted him with the money. Well, the Lord Jesus Christ has received the anointing as our Great High Priest in order to do the work of His priestly office. And one aspect of His work is to intercede. Therefore, He must be very willing to do it.

Again, the more people's proper work pertains also to those who are related to them, the more they are willing (if they are faithful) to do the work. Consider this a little. When people are exalted and come to greatness or honor, they share the comforts with their family, with those who depend on them. If a father gets a promotion, his children benefit. Well, the Lord Jesus Christ is our High Priest and is now exalted. He has gone to heaven. Therefore, His exaltation benefits all who stand related to Him. He is therefore very willing to work on our behalf.

Furthermore, intercession is the work of His office as priest. What people do in their offices, they do willingly. What people do in their offices, they do industriously; they do not do it by the by. What they do by their offices, they do readily.

People's perspectives will be according to their offices. For example, suppose that a very intelligent child came before three men of three professions: a lawyer, a minister, and a merchant. Referring to this intelligent child, the merchant says, "He will make a very good merchant." The lawyer says, "He will make a very good lawyer." And the minister says, "He will make a very good student." So their interpretations are according to their three offices or work. Or suppose that three different tradesmen, whose work involved wood, see a fine green tree. One man says, "It is good for this." Another says, "It is good for that." And the third says, "It is good for another use." So a person's perspective is according to their place and calling.

So now, when a poor soul comes before God, Moses (the law) looks upon him, the devil looks upon him, and Jesus Christ looks upon him. The work of the law is to condemn, the work of the devil is to accuse, and the work of Jesus Christ is to intercede. To intercede is the work of His office. Now therefore, as soon as the devil sees such a soul, he says, "Oh, here is a fine instrument for me; here is a fit subject for me to enjoy." As soon as Moses sees this man, he says, "Here is a fine subject for me to condemn to all eternity." But when Jesus Christ looks upon such a soul, He says, "Here is a fine soul for Me to save for all eternity, to intercede for!" Why? Because it is His office, and a man's perspective accords with his office. Therefore, what the Lord Jesus Christ does, He does by His office, and He does it readily and willingly.

I will give you one demonstration of this. The purpose for which Jesus Christ was taken into heaven, into the Most Holy Place, was that He might intercede. We know this according to the Scripture mentioned before, Hebrews 9:24: "For Christ has not entered the holy places made with hands, which are copies of the true, but into heaven itself, now to appear in the presence of

God for us." The author did not say, "Christ has now gone to heaven to be glorified there; Christ has now gone to heaven to enjoy the presence of His Father for His own happiness." No, but that He has gone into heaven "to appear in the presence of God for us." This is the purpose of His ascension.

And so again in Hebrews 7:25: "Therefore He is also able to save to the uttermost those who come to God through Him, since He always lives to make intercession for them." What! Is He in heaven only to be glorified there? No, Christ is in heaven to make intercession for poor sinners. Therefore, He must be infinitely willing to intercede because it is His purpose for going to heaven into the Most Holy Place. Oh therefore be of good comfort, all you who come to God through Him! For He is willing to intercede for you. Let not anything discourage you.

Perhaps you will complain, saying, "Oh, but I face much opposition here in this world." What does it matter, as long as Jesus Christ intercedes for you in heaven and speaks good words to God the Father for you in heaven?

Perhaps you will complain, saying, "Oh, but I am very tempted and cannot pray." Be humbled for it, yet know this: that when you cannot pray, Christ prays for you. And He prays that you might pray.

Perhaps you will complain, saying, "Oh, but I labor under such and such corruptions, and the devil is busy with me, exceedingly busy, and I cannot overcome them. And the devil stands at my right hand to tempt me and to lead me into such and such sins." Well, even if it is so, the Lord Jesus Christ is at the right hand of our Father. He has sat down at the right hand of God the Father till all His enemies are made to be His footstool. And your sins are His enemies. Therefore, be of good comfort, all you people of the Lord. Is there ever a poor myrtle tree in a hollow—a soul that grows in a poor dark condition? Be of good comfort, the Lord Jesus Christ, our Great High Priest, has entered into heaven, into the Most Holy Place, to intercede with God the Father for you.

Holiness
But you might say, "Does this lead to our grace and holiness too? And how does it?" Yes, this intercession of Jesus Christ, this work of His priestly office and our consideration of it, is very helpful to our grace and holiness.

For first, what a mighty encouragement this is for all poor sinners to come to Jesus Christ. Remember Hebrews 7:25: "He always lives to make intercession for them." And who is "them"? The beginning of the verse tells us it is "those who come to God through Him." Oh, then who would not come to God by Christ?

I think a poor sinner might say, "Indeed, my sins were so great that I was afraid to come to God. But now I hear that the Lord Jesus Christ is in heaven to make intercession for all those who come to God through

Him. Though I have been a drunkard, now I will go to
God through Christ. And though I have been a swearer
and though I have been unclean, yet I will go to God
through Christ. Indeed, I thought my time was past, for
I have been an old swearer, an old drunkard, and an old
Sabbath-breaker. I have been a sinner so long that I was
even afraid of going to God at all. I thought there was no
mercy and no pardon for me. But seeing now that this
is true, that the Lord Jesus Christ is in heaven to make
intercession for all those that come to God through Him,
well, through the Lord's grace, now I will go to the Lord
Jesus Christ. Indeed, I am a young man and a poor ignorant creature, and I thought there was no purpose for
going to God, that God would not regard poor ignorant,
ones. But now I understand that the Lord Jesus Christ is
in heaven to make intercession for all those that come to
God through Him. Well then, though I am ignorant, yet
I will go to God through Christ. And though I am but
a poor young person, and scarce understand the terms of
religion, yet I will go to God through Christ."

Oh, come to Christ, come to Christ! Behold here,
in the name of the Lord, I stand and make this invitation to poor sinners. Come, poor drunkard, swearer,
Sabbath-breaker, unclean heart! The Lord Jesus Christ
is in heaven to make intercession for all who come to
God through Him. Will you not come? Oh, how will
you answer it at the great day, when it shall be said, "The
Lord Jesus Christ made a tender offer of mercy to you,

and you would not accept it; you would not come to him"? Here is great encouragement to all poor sinners to come to Jesus Christ.

Second, the more I understand and see with a spiritual eye that the Lord Jesus Christ appears in heaven for me, the more am I engaged to appear upon earth for Him. I entreat you to mark how this leads to grace and holiness. Ah, shall the Lord Jesus Christ appear in heaven before saints and angels and God the Father for my soul, and shall I be afraid to appear before poor worms for Him? Shall the Lord Jesus Christ own me in heaven, and shall not I own Him upon earth? Shall the Lord Jesus Christ, as the Great High Priest, take my name and carry it upon His breast into the presence of God the Father, and shall not I take the name of Christ and hold it forth to the world? Oh, I beseech you to consider what a mighty engagement this is to stand and appear for the Lord Christ and to own His cause in these backsliding times, because He is now in heaven appearing for you and making intercession for you!

Third, the more I consider that the Lord Jesus Christ lay Himself out for me, the more engaged I will be to lay myself out for Him. The Scripture says, "He always lives to make intercession for them" (Heb. 7:25). He lays out His whole eternity for you. I think we have here the greatest argument in the world to make us walk closely with God in Christ. For shall the Lord Jesus Christ spend His eternity for me, and shall not I

spend my whole time for Him? "He *always* lives to make
intercession" (emphasis added). Before the world was
made, His delight was in the habitable parts of the earth,
among the children of men. Well, in due time He came
down into the world. And while here upon the earth,
He laid Himself out fully for you. Then He died and
went up to heaven, having said, "I go to prepare a place
for you" (John 14:2). He was at work for you before the
world began; then He came down to the earth and here
spent all His time for you; and now that He has gone to
heaven, the text says, "He always lives to make intercession for [you]." He spends all His eternity for you. Oh,
the Lord Jesus does not begrudge to spend eternity for
my soul! Shall I begrudge to spend a little time for Him?

Surely people do not think about what Christ is
doing in heaven for them, especially those who are saints.
If they did, they could not be dabbling in the world so
much. Shall the Lord Jesus Christ be appearing in heaven
for me, and shall I be digging in the world? Shall He be
mentioning my name to God the Father and interceding for me, and shall I be sinning against Him? Shall I
be contending with His children? Shall I now be joining
with His enemies? Shall I be opposing His ways?

Oh, if people would but think about what the Lord
Jesus Christ is doing for them in heaven, they would not
rebel against Him in the world as they do! Therefore,
that you may be kept from your sins, and kept from the
world, think of these things. The apostle says, "These

things I write to you, so that you may not sin. And if anyone sins, we have an Advocate with the Father, Jesus Christ the righteous" (1 John 2:1). And so I say to you: I have been here delivering to you this doctrine concerning the priestly office of Jesus Christ, and these things have I preached to you so that you might not sin. And therefore, that you may be kept from sin and your hearts made more holy, think of the priestly office of Jesus Christ. He has gone into heaven to make intercession for you.

CHAPTER 4

Offering Gifts

We have already learned that the work of the high priest was and now is to provide satisfaction and intercession for the sins of the people. If we further inquire, we will also find that the work of the high priest was and now is to offer the people's gifts to God: to present our prayers, praises, duties, services, and all spiritual duties to God the Father and to obtain their acceptance.

This is how it was done. In the times of Moses, there were courts in the tabernacle (see Hebrews 9). The ark, the mercy seat, the cherubim of glory, and the golden censer were in the inner court, called the Most Holy Place. In the outer court were the brazen altar upon which they offered sacrifices, the table of showbread, the golden candlestick, and the golden altar upon which they offered incense. This is clearly described in Hebrews 9:2–5:

> For a tabernacle was prepared: the first part, in which was the lampstand, the table, and the

showbread, which is called the sanctuary; and behind the second veil, the part of the tabernacle which is called the Holiest of All, which had the golden censer and the ark of the covenant overlaid on all sides with gold, in which were the golden pot that had the manna, Aaron's rod that budded, and the tablets of the covenant; and above it were the cherubim of glory overshadowing the mercy seat.

And just as a lamb was offered daily on the brazen altar every morning and evening, as sacrifice for the sins of the people, so incense was offered daily each morning and evening on the golden altar. This was done while the people outside were praying, so that the incense was sweetly mingled together with their prayers, as we see in Luke 1:8–10: "So it was, that while he [Zacharias] was serving as priest before God in the order of his division, according to the custom of the priesthood, his lot fell to burn incense when he went into the temple of the Lord. And the whole multitude of the people was praying outside at the hour of incense."

And though a sacrifice was made every day, yet once a year the high priest took the blood of the sacrifice, carried it into the Most Holy Place, and sprinkled it on the mercy seat. And although incense was offered daily on the golden altar, yet only once a year did the high priest take the golden censer, with incense from the golden altar, and bring it into the Most Holy Place, causing a cloud of perfume to arise on the mercy seat.

All of this was a great type of Jesus Christ, our High Priest. Though He offered Himself once as the sacrifice for sin, yet when He died and ascended, He carried the virtue of His blood into the Most Holy Place in heaven and sprinkled the mercy seat with it. Although He began to intercede while He lived (as we read in John 17), when He ascended up to the Most Holy Place in heaven, He took His golden censer and carried His intercession into heaven, causing a cloud of sweet perfumes to arise upon the mercy seat. He still does this, while we are here praying without His bodily presence—He mingles all our duties with His intercessions, and so takes them together as one and presents it to God the Father for our acceptance. And this He does now as our High Priest. For when we look in the book of Hebrews, we find that the apostle, speaking of the High Priest and relating to Jesus Christ, says that His work is to "offer both gifts and sacrifices for sins" (Heb. 5:1). We read in Hebrews 8:3 that every high priest is appointed to offer both gifts and sacrifices. We thus have another great work of our Great High Priest—namely, to offer up all our prayers, duties, and gifts to God the Father. We could call this another part of Christ's intercession, but I will handle it distinctly.

In order to clearly explain this great gospel mystery, I will show five things:

1. how Jesus Christ as our High Priest offers up our gifts to God the Father;

2. the abundance of favor and acceptance our
   Great High Priest Himself has in heaven;

3. how He uses His own acceptance to secure our
   acceptance, planting all our duties upon the
   acceptance He has with the Father;

4. the abundant acceptance we thus have through
   Him in all our duties; and

5. how this leads to our comfort and holiness.

Christ Offers Our Gifts

What does Jesus Christ as our High Priest do in offering up our gifts to God the Father? First, He takes our
persons and brings them in to God the Father, in a way
that is most imperceptible to us. He knows that if our
persons are not first accepted, then our duties cannot be
accepted. Love me, and then love my duty; love me, and
then love my service. Hate me, and then hate my service.

In the covenant of works, God first accepted the work
and then the person. He accepted the person for his or
her work. But in the covenant of grace, God first accepts
the person and then the work. Therefore, in order for
our works and duties to be accepted by God the Father,
the Lord Christ, our High Priest, first takes our person
and name, and carries them into the presence of God the
Father. This was plainly shadowed by the high priest in
the Old Testament, who went into the Most Holy Place
with the names of all the tribes on his breastplate.

The apostle Paul clearly speaks of our acceptance when he says, "In whom we have boldness and access with confidence through faith in Him" (Eph. 3:12). The word *access*, as some have observed, suggests the idea of leading someone by the hand. Thus this verse could be translated, "In whom we have a hand-leading," or "By whom we are led by the hand to God the Father." As a child, having run away from his father, is taken by the hand of a friend or his elder brother and brought again into the presence of his father, so we, having all run away from God, are taken and led again into the presence of the Father by the hand of Jesus Christ. He is the ladder that Jacob saw, upon whom we do ascend into the presence of God and go into heaven. Thus, our High Priest, Jesus Christ, first takes our persons and leads us into the presence of God the Father.

Second, as He takes our persons and carries us into the presence of God the Father, so, when we perform any duty, He observes what evil or failing is in the duty and draws it out. He takes it away before He presents the duty to God the Father. A child, wanting to give his father a bouquet of flowers, goes into the garden and gathers flowers and weeds together. But then he comes to his mother, and she picks out the weeds, binds the flowers by themselves, and then presents it to the father. So it is with us—when we go to perform a duty, we gather weeds and flowers together. But the Lord Jesus

Christ picks out the weeds and then presents nothing but flowers to God the Father.

We see this in Exodus 28, when the high priest bears the iniquity of the holy things of God's people. In verses 36–37, we read:

> You shall also make a plate of pure gold and engrave on it, like the engraving of a signet:
>
> HOLINESS TO THE LORD.
>
> And you shall put it on a blue cord, that it may be on the turban; it shall be on the front of the turban.

Then in verse 38: "So it shall be on Aaron's forehead, that Aaron may bear the iniquity of the holy things which the children of Israel hallow in all their holy gifts; and it shall always be on his forehead, that they may be accepted before the LORD."

Then, clearly referring to our Savior Christ (see v. 1), we read in Malachi 3:2–4:

> But who can endure the day of His coming?
> And who can stand when He appears?
> For He is like a refiner's fire
> And like launderers' soap.
> He will sit as a refiner and a purifier of silver;
> He will purify the sons of Levi,
> And purge them as gold and silver,
> That they may offer to the LORD
> An offering in righteousness.

Then the offering of Judah and Jerusalem
Will be pleasant to the LORD,
As in the days of old,
As in former years.

Malachi said that then their offering "will be pleasant." When? When He has purged their sacrifices and offerings. This is what our Lord Christ our Great High Priest does in offering up our gifts to God the Father. He takes out the weeds. He purges and takes away the iniquity of our holy things.

Third, as He takes away the iniquity of our holy things, He also observes whatever is good in our duties and mingles it together with the incense of His intercession, presenting it all to God the Father as one work mingled together. We see this fully in Revelation 8:3–4: "Then another angel, having a golden censer, came and stood at the altar. He was given much incense, that he should offer it with the prayers of all the saints upon the golden altar which was before the throne. And the smoke of the incense, with the prayers of the saints, ascended before God from the angel's hand." The angel must refer to Christ, for angels do not intercede but only Christ, who is called the angel of the covenant (Mal. 3:1). It says that "having a golden censer," He came and "stood at the altar." No one but the high priest had a golden censer. He was given much incense, and this he offered with the prayers of all the saints, so that the smoke of the incense ascended up before the Lord with the prayers of the saints. This allusion to the custom of the Jewish high priest clearly shows us what the Lord Jesus Christ, as our Great High Priest, does for us in offering up our gifts to God the Father.

The Beloved Son

Second, what abundance of favor and acceptance does our Great High Priest have in heaven? He has very much. He said, "Father, I thank You that You have heard Me. And I know that You always hear Me" (John 11:41–42). We read, as I remember, of only two places in the New Testament where the Father gives testimony to Jesus Christ, His Son, by an audible voice, and in both places the same words are given: "This is My beloved Son, in whom I am well pleased" (Matt. 3:17; 17:5).[1]

We may know how much favor one man has with another by the trust that is committed to him. Joseph had great favor in the eyes of Pharaoh. How was this seen? Because Pharaoh entrusted him with so much. Now God the Father has entrusted Jesus Christ, our Great High Priest, with very much. I will show this in four instances.

---

1. Bridge evidently forgot about John 12:27–28:

Now My soul is troubled, and what shall I say? "Father, save Me from this hour"? But for this purpose I came to this hour. Father, glorify Your name.

Then a voice came from heaven, saying, "I have both glorified it and will glorify it again."

First, consider the agreement made before the foundation of the world between God the Father and Christ, the second person of the Trinity. They agreed that in due time, Christ would come into the world, become flesh, and die for sinners, and He did this. But thousands of souls were saved before Christ came into the world. How were they saved? They were saved by the blood of Christ, yet before Christ had died. So then, God the Father saved them upon Christ's bare word—His agreement to come into the world and die for them. What a mighty trust this was! So many hundreds of thousands of souls would be saved upon the bare word of Christ that He would afterward come into the world and die for them.

Again, the trust appears in this—that Christ, when He came into the world, was made the great Lord Treasurer of all the grace and comfort that would be given to the children of men. When Pharaoh trusted Joseph, the whole kingdom was put into his hands, including the corn and grain, so that nothing was to be given out to anyone apart from Joseph. This showed a mighty trust. And now there is no grace or comfort given out to the children of men, apart from the hand of Christ. This shows what a mighty trust the Father has given Him.

Further, when our Lord and Savior Christ died, He ascended to God the Father in heaven. As soon as He came into heaven, the Father acknowledged Christ's suffering. Perhaps He even said:

Ask of Me, and I will give You
The nations for Your inheritance,
and the ends of the earth for Your possession.
   (Ps. 2:8)

God the Father would have told Jesus, "Ask of Me,
and at the first word I will give You the whole world." It
was a great and mighty trust the Father gave Jesus.

And, as if this were not enough, the Father placed
the keys of heaven and hell into the hands of Christ. So,
we read in Revelation 1:18: "I am He who lives, and was
dead, and behold, I am alive forevermore. Amen. And I
have the keys of Hades and of Death." No person goes
to hell but is locked in by Jesus Christ; and no person
goes to heaven but Christ has the keys and locks each
person in for all eternity. The Lord Jesus Christ has the
keys of heaven and hell. He has the keys of all people's
eternity hanging at His belt. Oh, what an infinite trust
that God the Father has given Him!

Accepted in the Beloved

Third, does He use His own acceptance to secure our
acceptance, planting all our duties upon the acceptance He has with the Father? Yes, Christ improves
all His favor and acceptance for our acceptance. He
plants our prayers and duties upon His own acceptance. Concerning believers, He prayed, "Father,
I desire that they also whom You gave Me may be
with Me where I am.... [I desire] that they all may

be one, as You, Father, are in Me, and I in You; that they also may be one in Us" (John 17:24, 21, respectively). He does not count Himself full and happy apart from the fullness and happiness of the church. For the church "is His body, the fullness of Him who fills all in all" (Eph. 1:23). When our Lord and Savior Christ came to die, He shows in His prayer in John 17 that He prays not so much for Himself but rather intercedes for believers.

In the time of Moses, the high priest's favor and acceptance was not for himself but for the people. He was clothed in priestly garments: a turban upon his head and a golden ephod about his waist. Wearing these, he was accepted when he came into the Most Holy Place. But he came not for himself but for the people. And our High Priest, Jesus Christ, goes beyond all other high priests in this as well. For they only went into the Most Holy Place once a year, but our High Priest is always in the Most Holy Place. He never departs but is always covering the mercy seat with His intercessions. More than that, the high priests in the Old Testament, as holy as they were, sometimes made the people naked and unacceptable (see the golden calf incident in Exodus 32). But our Great High Priest never makes His people naked; He always clothes them in His own righteousness.

And though their high priest went into the Most Holy Place for the people, he never led the people themselves inside. They stood without. Yet our Great High

Priest has not only gone into the Most Holy Place Himself, but He leads every poor believer inside as well. For we read in Hebrews 10:19: "Therefore, brethren, having boldness to enter the Holiest by the blood of Jesus."

So, if our Great High Priest in this respect goes beyond all the high priests who ever went before Him, and if they improved their interest, favor, and acceptance for the sake of the people, then how much more does the Lord Jesus Christ, our High Priest, improve His favor, interest, and acceptance in heaven for our sakes to secure our acceptance and the acceptance of all our duties.

Our Duties Accepted

Fourth, do we really have great acceptance in all our duties through Him? Yes, we have very great acceptance in and through our High Priest, the Lord Jesus Christ. That is why our Lord and Savior says, "And whatever you ask in My name, that I will do" (John 14:13). Yes, but can we be sure of this? He repeats it again in verse 14: "If you ask anything in My name, I will do it." Yes, so that we may see the great acceptance we now have through Him in all the duties we offer up to God the Father, Jesus said, "In that day you will ask in My name, and I do not say to you that I shall pray the Father for you; for the Father Himself loves you" (John 16:26–27). This is a mighty and high statement—"I do not say that I shall pray for you. You have so much favor and love in heaven, from the Father himself, that He will hear you."

Yes, but is this not all upon Christ's account? Yes, and therefore, He said, "And whatever you ask in My name, that I will do, that the Father may be glorified in the Son" (John 14:13). All is given upon Christ's account.

The testimony of Christ's acceptance from heaven was great. "This is My beloved Son, in whom I am well pleased" (Matt. 3:17). Now, if we look in Scripture, we shall find that the same words are given to the saints. The Lord Jesus Christ is called the Son of God—"My beloved Son"—and so are believers: "But as many as received him, to them gave he power to become the sons of God" (John 1:12 KJV). Jesus Christ is called the *beloved* Son of God," and so are the saints: "Is Ephraim [Israel] My dear son? Is he a pleasant child?" (Jer. 31:20). In reference to Jesus Christ, God the Father also said, "In whom I am well pleased." This same word is also given to men. When our Lord and Savior Christ was born into the world, the angels came and sang at His birth, "Goodwill toward men" (Luke 2:14)—or "men with whom he is well pleased," the same word used concerning Christ Himself. So, then, every word in this statement, "My beloved Son, in whom I am well pleased" is given also to the saints, to believers. This shows how greatly Christ improves His own favor and acceptance for our acceptance. This is the great acceptance we have through Christ.

Yes, as the Lord Jesus Christ is said (abstractly speaking) to be made sin for us, so also we are said to be made righteousness in Him (2 Cor. 5:21). The saints and believers are called "righteousness." So then, here is the great acceptance that the saints and believers find through the acceptance of Jesus Christ our Great High Priest.

But suppose a man is very poor and lives in some poor cottage, which has only one room to eat and sleep in and that room is dark and smoky too. And suppose this poor creature comes and prays to God. Will the great and glorious God of heaven and earth take notice of such a prayer, from such a worm as this? Shall he find acceptance with God the Father?

For the answer, look at the Song of Solomon 2:14, which are the words of Christ speaking to the church:

> O my dove, in the clefts of the rock,
> In the secret places of the cliff,
> Let me see your face,
> Let me hear your voice;
> For your voice is sweet,
> And your face is lovely.

I ask, where now is the church? "In the clefts of the rock" and "in the secret places of the cliff"—in other words, in a poor distressed place, a hidden place. And now, He says their voice is sweet and their face is lovely.

Well, suppose that a person weak in grace—someone weak in abilities and gifts—performs some service and duty. For some will say, "That is my case; I am of very meager abilities and gifts. I have little memory and little ability to speak. There are some indeed who have great gifts and graces, and when they pray, I don't question that their prayers are accepted. But as for me, my abilities are meager and small. Oh, can there be any acceptance through Jesus Christ for prayers such as mine? Will God answer such stammering, lisping, imperfect, broken, and half-spoken petitions as mine?"

Yes, for we know that in the time of the law a pair of turtledoves were accepted on behalf of those who could offer no more. Surely, much more now in the time of the gospel, a poor "turtledove" will be accepted by God. Even those who could only bring goats' hair to contribute to building the tabernacle were welcomed! How much more will poor gifts be welcomed now in gospel times! What is little in terms of quantity may be great in terms of proportion. Such was the widow's mites (Mark 12:42).

We know that the sun shines with common influence on all herbs and plants, though they vary in their sweetness and growth. The violet is not as tall as the rose, yet it has its own sweetness and may say to the rose, "Though I am not as tall as you, yet I have my sweetness as well as you." So now, there is a common influence from Jesus Christ upon all the saints, though they vary in sweetness and growth. One is like the rose, another like the violet. Perhaps here lies a poor Christian upon the ground like the violet, one that is not as tall in gifts and graces as another; yet, notwithstanding, this person has his or her sweetness. Christ lovingly receives that which comes from love, whatever it is, no matter how weak it is.

Well, suppose a person's duty and service is performed with much failure, infirmity, hardness of heart, narrowness of spirit, and distracting thoughts? "This is my case," one says. "Oh, is there any acceptance for a duty such as this? Will the Lord Jesus Christ, the Great High Priest, receive such a duty as this and carry it to God the Father?"

We know how it was with Nicodemus and with the woman who came trembling to touch the hem of Christ's garment. And we must know that in every duty we perform, there are two things: there is the sacrifice itself, and there is the obedience in offering the sacrifice. And though the sacrifice is imperfect, yet your obedience in offering the sacrifice may be perfect with gospel-perfection. God deals with duties as He deals with persons. Never think that God will deal otherwise with our duties than He does with our persons. When the Lord justified you, He was justifying the ungodly. He came and found a poor soul in a sinful condition, imputed His righteousness to that soul, and justified the ungodly, though not so that person would continue in sin. As the apostle said, Jesus Christ "justifies the ungodly" (Rom. 4:5). So the Lord comes and finds a great deal of ungodliness in your duty, and He imputes His righteousness to that duty and so justifies the duty, which in your eyes is an ungodly duty.

This indeed is a wonder that He should deal with us in this way. Did we ever hear of a garment that would make the crooked straight? If a man has a crooked back, and someone comes and puts velvet, silk, or scarlet upon him, it might make him more handsome, but it will not change his back and make him straight. But when the Lord Christ came, He found all our souls as crooked backs, as it were, and put His righteousness upon us. And this garment makes straight that which was crooked. It makes the very crook-backed duty to become a straight duty.

Did we ever hear or read of any seal, that when set upon the wax, could change the wax to gold or silver? The seal may leave its impression, but it does not change the wax into its own metal. When a stamp is set upon silver or gold, the metal remains as it was before. If a stamp is set upon brass, it does not turn it to silver; or if it is set upon silver, it does not turn it to gold. Yes, but when the Lord Jesus Christ comes to a duty and sets His own stamp upon it—when He sets His own righteousness upon a duty—that which was brass before (that is, full of failure and much unrighteousness) turns into gold or silver! Christ alone has the philosopher's stone (if I may so speak), so that all He touches turns to gold. He turns our duties into gold. And when He has done so, He presents them to God the Father. This is what our Great High Priest does.

Our Comfort and Holiness

Comfort

Surely we can already see how it leads to our comfort. Isn't it comforting for people to know that their duties are not lost? That their prayers are not lost? That their hearing of the word is not lost? That their searching of the Scriptures is not lost? That their conversation and fellowship with others is not lost? People are not willing to lose anything, and the more precious it is, the less they are willing to lose it. If we have a venture at sea, we are unwilling to lose our venture; and the greater our venture is, the less willing we are to lose it. If people have one-fourth of their belongings on a ship, they are not willing to lose it. They are less willing if it is half of their estate, and they are most unwilling if everything they own, as well as their children, are on the ship. Now as people are unwilling to lose their worldly venture, so people who are sensible of their souls are very unwilling to lose their soul's ventures: to lose their prayers and all their duties.

Friends, here is an insuring office; the Lord Jesus Christ is our great insurer in this respect. And He does as He is our High Priest, offering up our gifts to God the Father, assuring us that nothing is lost. Indeed, if we had the kind of high priest who was unable to take notice of the circumstances of our duties, we might lose much. But the Lord Christ, our Great High Priest, takes notice not only of our duties, whatever they are, but of all the circumstances of our duties too. And these He presents to God the Father, in all their gracious circumstances. Therefore, He said to the angel of the church of Pergamos in Revelation 2:13, "I know your works." Perhaps you might say, "But Lord, though You know my works, yet perhaps You do not take notice where my work is done. Maybe You take notice of my prayer, but do not take notice of my family and dwelling place. Lord, I am in a wicked, wretched family that opposes prayer. Lord, maybe You take notice of my prayer, but do not take notice of this circumstance." Yes, but if we read the entire verse, we see that Christ said, "I know your works, and where you dwell, where Satan's throne is. And you hold fast to My name, and did not deny My faith even in the days in which Antipas was My faithful martyr, who was killed among you, where Satan dwells."

This is remarkable: the Lord Jesus Christ takes notice not only of our duties but of every circumstance of our duties, and so presents them both to God the Father. Therefore, not a hair of your duty is lost, nor one grain of your duty. Isn't this an unspeakable comfort to a poor soul, to know that nothing of all one's prayers to God are lost? The very longings of our hearts at the throne of grace are received into the heart of our heavenly Father.

Furthermore, isn't it a comfort to have freedom to go to the mercy seat to meet with God? It is said of wicked men that they sit in the seat of the scornful (Ps. 1:1). There is, it seems, the seat of the scornful and there is a mercy seat. A drunkard, when with his drunken company, sits upon the ale bench, scorning and jeering at the godly, making up songs about them: he sits in the seat of the scornful, a cursed seat. Yes, but there is another seat: there is a mercy seat, and any poor saint, any child of God, may go in to the mercy seat of the Lord Jesus Christ, having all the favor and acceptance of heaven. He carries that soul in to the mercy seat, and God the Father will never set Christ or the child He carries aside. What comfort this is!

Besides, is it not a great comfort for people to know how it will go for them at the great day of judgment? When there shall be hundreds of thousands at the right hand of Christ and hundreds of thousands at the left hand of Christ—when all faces shall grow pale? "Oh!" one says. "If I could only know how it shall go for me on that day!" This doctrine tells us that the Lord Jesus Christ is our judge on that day—He who takes our prayers and duties now and carries them into the presence of God the Father. By Him we have acceptance, and according to these, we shall be judged. So then, if He takes your duties and carries them to God the Father for acceptance, He will surely never judge you for them or condemn you for them at that day. Here is comfort!

Once more, isn't it comforting for a poor beggar to find relief at a rich person's door? We are all beggars in relation to heaven. And the Lord Jesus Christ not only comes forth to serve us, but He takes us poor beggars by the hand and leads us in heaven to His Father. Oh, what comfort is here! What comfort is here!

Indeed, if I could say that the Lord accepts my duty, that would be comfort indeed. If I could conclude that the Lord Jesus Christ took my prayer and duties and carried them in to God the Father, this would be a sweet consolation. But shall I know that?

If the Lord Jesus Christ is our High Priest, then we may also say that He carries our duties in to God the Father for acceptance. If we can say that Jesus Christ has offered satisfaction for us and intercedes for us, then we may also say that He carries our duties to God the Father for acceptance.

Furthermore, to bring comfort nearer to your hearts, let me appeal to you: whoever you are who makes this objection, did you ever find a spiritual fire come down from heaven (as it were) upon your heart in or after doing your duty? In the Old Testament, if they offered a sacrifice and fire came down from heaven to burn the sacrifice to ashes, it was a certain testimony that the sacrifice was accepted. Now, in the times of the gospel, we must not expect literal fire to come upon our duties. But has the Lord ever caused an inward, spiritual fire to fall upon your heart, warming your spirit before or after your duty? There the Lord speaks much to you—your sacrifice is turned to ashes and accepted by Jesus Christ.

Or do you who make this objection ever have it in your heart to cry out in prayer and intercession for others, especially the godly? Look, Christ has the same disposition in His heart toward you, as you have toward His members. Ah! Do you think there is love in your heart toward the saints yet there is none in Christ's heart toward you? Do you think your compassion is larger than Christ's? If you can find it in your heart to cry out to God in prayer and intercession when you see a saint in misery, do you not think that the Lord Jesus has as great compassion toward you, to intercede for you and present your prayers to God the Father?

Furthermore, do you look upon your own duties, which come from yourself, as most unworthy? Beloved! It is in regard to duties as it is in regard to persons. When a person judges himself or herself to be most unworthy, then Christ counts that person worthy. And God counts that person worthy in Christ. As you read in Song of Solomon 1:5–6, when the spouse said,

> I am dark, but lovely,
> O daughters of Jerusalem,
> Like the tents of Kedar....
> Do not look upon me, because I am dark.

But though she counts herself dark, Christ's opinion of her is seen in verse 8, the "fairest among women." Now, when people count themselves as most unworthy, God counts them as most worthy. When people look upon their own duties and sacrifices as most unworthy, they are looked upon by Jesus Christ as most worthy. What are poor prayers in our eyes are precious in God's.

One more word: Don't you think that grace is greater now in gospel times than it was in times of the law? If you doubt it, look at the altar in Exodus 30:1–2 (under the law), compared with the altar in Ezekiel 41:22 (under the gospel). The altar of incense in gospel times was to be larger than the altar under the law. In the Old Testament, in the time of law, poor souls could go to the high priest and say that their services, duties, and sacrifices were accepted by the high priest. How much more may poor souls now go to Jesus Christ, our Great High Priest, and say that their services, duties, and sacrifices have been accepted through Him? Here is an abundance of comfort for the saints. Be of good comfort, all you who believe!

Holiness

But how does this lead to holiness in our lives? We confess, indeed, that there is abundant comfort in knowing that the Lord Jesus Christ, our Great High Priest, takes all our gifts and prayers and presents them to God the Father, and that we have acceptance in His acceptance. But does this lead to holiness in our lives?

Much, in every way!

First, if I am an ungodly, wicked person, Christ's work as my High Priest overcomes my opposition to the good ways of God. A wicked person might say, "I have sometimes accused the godly in their duties of hypocrisy and pride. And with bitterness and earnestness I have opposed the praying and striving of God's people. But if it is true that the Lord Jesus Christ takes the prayers of God's least children and carries them into the bosom of God the Father, shall I then spit upon that which Christ owns? Shall I dare oppose that which the Lord Jesus Christ presents to His Father? May the Lord in mercy pardon me! I have sinned and done foolishly, for I have spoken evil of the duty that Christ has carried into the presence of God the Father. Oh, through the Lord's grace, then, I will forever cease my opposition against the good ways of God! I will never again speak a word against the persons, meetings, and supplications of the godly."

This is also a further encouragement for the ungodly, wicked person to come to Jesus Christ; yes, and to come quickly. For is not Jesus Christ Jacob's ladder, by whom we go up to heaven? Does He not take all our duties and prayers and present them to God the Father for acceptance? Then, all is nothing and all is lost until I come to Christ. If I am a drunkard and will not come to Christ, all prayer is lost. If I am a swearer or an unclean wretch and will not come to Christ, then all my prayers and duties are lost. Oh, may the Lord pity me that I already lost too many prayers! Now, through the Lord's grace, I will lose no more. Oh, come to Christ! Lord, I come, I come. This is a mighty encouragement for every man to quickly come to Jesus Christ. For the

Lord Jesus Christ, our High Priest, takes every duty and carries it into the bosom of God the Father for acceptance. So, this is an encouragement for the ungodly.

Second, this truth leads to my further holiness if I am godly. For here I see an infinite reason for attending to my duty—not only to pray but to pray often. Why? Because the Lord Jesus Christ carries it all into the bosom of the Father. He mingles the aroma of His intercessions with my prayer, even if it is just a sigh or groan. Thus, the apostle said, "Let us therefore come boldly to the throne of grace" (Heb. 4:16). The word *boldly* means to speak all one's mind—let us come speaking all. Having such a High Priest, who will carry every sign and groan into the presence of God the Father for acceptance, who then would not often be in prayer? Speak all to Christ. Be free with Christ. Come with boldness!

Many poor souls are greatly discouraged and dare not pray. They often fear to go to the throne of grace. The reason is because they look upon their prayers or duties as they lie upon their own hearts, as if it comes from themselves. But, my beloved, your prayers and duties are like fire. There is much smoke and ash with your fire upon the hearth but not in the element of fire itself. So it is with your prayer—when it lies upon your own hearth, there is much smoke. But once it gets into the hands of Jesus Christ, there is its element and it is freed from all its smoke. Or think of a man's body. As long as he lives upon the earth, he is feeble and weak and often sick. But when he comes into heaven, all his weakness is taken away and soon his glorified body will be made strong. All diseases will be gone. So it is with our prayers—as long as they are here below, in our own hearts, they are full of weakness, but as soon as our prayers are spoken, they are in the hands of Christ in heaven, and the weakness is taken away. Oh, it is a glorified prayer, once it is in the hands of Christ! Therefore, this is a great encouragement for the godly not only to be in prayer but to be in prayer often. Come with boldness to the throne of grace.

Again, if you are godly—indeed, even if you are ungodly—here is an infinite reason to receive every truth that comes from Christ, though it is spoken by one with many failures. The Lord Jesus Christ accepts every prayer and duty that comes from me, though they have many weaknesses; indeed, He takes my prayer and carries it into the presence of God the Father for acceptance. So then, when a truth comes from Christ, shall I not accept it? Even though the minister or preacher who speaks it labors with this or that weakness? Perhaps there is pride or some other miscarriage in his delivery. But if the Lord Christ shall accept my prayers with all their infirmities, shall not I accept Christ's truth, notwithstanding the infirmities of the poor messenger who brings it?

Third, the more evangelical you are in your obedience, the more holy you are in your lives. This truth that is now before you, when well studied and considered, will make you more obedient in an evangelical way. You therefore find that the Lord Himself from heaven makes this use of it. Consult with Matthew 17:5: "This is My beloved Son, in whom I am well pleased. Hear Him!" In the phrase "Hear Him," hearing implies faith and obedience, not merely hearing with the ears. Compare this with Matthew 3:17: "And suddenly a voice came from heaven, saying, 'This is My beloved Son, in whom I am well pleased.'" The phrase "Hear Him" is not in Matthew 3 but is in Matthew 17. Why is it included in one but not the other? Let me suggest reasons that relate to this discussion—not to mention the fact that Moses appeared with Elijah in Matthew 17, and that Moses, speaking of the prophet the Lord God would raise up, said, "Hear Him" (see Deut. 18:15).

The emphasis may be in the word "hear." "This is my beloved Son, in whom I am well pleased. *Hear* Him!" (emphasis added). Christ had appeared here in great glory. His face shined like the sun, His clothes were as white as light, and the disciples stood there gazing upon Him. But the Lord from heaven essentially said, "Do not just gaze upon Him, but hear Him. Listen to Him."

Furthermore, Moses and Elijah appeared here in Matthew 17 at the Transfiguration (v. 3). Moses had given the law, and Elijah had restored it. Peter then said, "Lord, it is good for us to be here; if You wish, let us make here three tabernacles: one for You, one for Moses, and one for Elijah" (v. 4). Peter treated Jesus, Moses, and Elijah equally—one tabernacle for each. And to correct

Peter in this mistake, God the Father essentially said, "Your eye is upon Moses, but I am well pleased with My Son—'This is My beloved Son in whom I am well pleased.' And I am pleased with you and your duties only through my Son, not through Moses. Therefore—'Hear Him!'—hear Christ, not Moses." In other words, He showed them they should be evangelical and hear Jesus Christ, because it is through Christ they have acceptance. Through Christ, God is well pleased with them.

Furthermore, the more Christ appears in glory, the greater reason we have to hear Him. The Lord Jesus Christ appeared here in glory, with His face shining like the sun and His garments white as light. He didn't appear in such glory in Matthew 3, when He was baptized, but He did here. Therefore, the Lord said, "Hear Him!" This is your glorious Savior—"Hear Him!" Beloved, in what greater glory can Jesus Christ appear to your souls than the glory of His love? He takes all of your duties and prayers and carries them to the bosom of God the Father so that by Him you have acceptance. Oh, what a glorious Savior you have! Therefore, hear Him! This of all things should make you obedient to Christ, over Moses. This should make you evangelical in all your duties.

Fourth, the more people can rejoice in spiritual privileges with humility, the more holy they are. A holy person is humble and yet able to rejoice in spiritual privileges. It takes great holiness to join these two things together. There are some who rejoice in their spiritual privileges but do not walk humbly. Others labor to walk humbly but are greatly troubled in consideration of their own sins; they do not rejoice in the spiritual privileges. Give me a Christian who can do both, and this is a blessed person. The study of the truth now before you will teach you to do both. For it is a great privilege that the Lord Christ carries every sigh, groan, and duty into the presence of God the Father, and presents it for us, and gives us acceptance. Considering this gives us great reason for joy. Yes, it is Christ who does this, and there is no worthiness in our duties, so that if Jesus Christ did not carry them in His hands into the presence of God the Father, they would be lost and cast away—so should we not therefore walk humbly?

I conclude with this: if the Lord Jesus Christ our Great High Priest offers up all our gifts to God the Father, whereby we have acceptance, what infinite cause we all have to be thankful to God for Christ and to love Jesus Christ forever!

Suppose one of you had been among the disciples when the Lord Christ washed His disciples' feet. Suppose He came and washed your feet. Would not your heart have glowed with love for Jesus Christ? Yet when the Lord Jesus Christ washed His disciples' feet, it was in the days of His flesh when He was here on the earth. But now He is in glory, and yet He takes your dirty prayers and (as it were) washes the feet of your prayers so that He may present them to God the Father. He washes your tears in His blood and presents them to God the Father. He takes all your duties and perfumes them with His intercessions, and so He presents them to God the Father. Oh, what cause we have to love Jesus Christ! Oh, you who never loved Christ, love Him now! And you who loved Him before, love Him now much more! You who fear the Lord, love the Lord! Let us all go blessing and praising the name of the Lord, with our hearts warmed by this love.

CHAPTER 5

Blessing the People

We have already studied and applied the three parts of the work of our High Priest: to make satisfaction for the sins of the people, to make intercession for them, and to offer up their gifts to God the Father. Now I shall speak of one more work of our Great High Priest: to bless the people.

In the Old Testament, we read of two sorts of high priests. One was according to the order of Aaron, the Levitical high priest. Part of his work was to bless the people, as we read in Numbers 6:23, when the Lord said to Moses, "Speak to Aaron and his sons, saying, 'This is the way you shall bless the children of Israel. Say to them.'" There was another high priest who was not according to this order of Aaron. This other high priest was Melchizedek, who blessed Abraham. The apostle, speaking of him as a great type of Jesus Christ, our Great High Priest, said in Hebrews 7:6 that he "received tithes from Abraham and blessed him." So we see that blessing the people was the work of both high priests, Aaron and Melchizedek, both of whom are great types of Jesus Christ, our High Priest. To bless the people must surely then be one of the great works of our High Priest.

To clearly explain this truth, I will endeavor to show five things:

1. the blessing that Christ, our High Priest, gives and what Christ does when He blesses the people;

2. that it especially belongs to Jesus Christ to bless the people;

3. that our Lord and Savior Christ, our Great High Priest, is greatly willing to bless poor sinners, and that He is very inclined and greatly delighted in this work of blessing the people;

4. that He does this work and does it fully;

5. how all this leads to our comfort and holiness.

Blessed with All Spiritual Blessings in Christ

What blessing does Christ, our High Priest, give and what does Christ do when He blesses the people? I answer first, in general, that the blessing of Christ and the gospel especially consists in spiritual things, rather than temporal. And therefore, the apostle said in Ephesians 1:3: "Blessed be the God and Father of our Lord Jesus Christ, who has blessed us with every spiritual blessing in the heavenly places in Christ." Under the gospel, the curse and judgments of God that befall men are not so much outward, bodily afflictions but are spiritual miseries, such as blindness of mind and hardness of heart. So also, the blessing of the gospel does not consist so much in outward things but in spiritual. He has "blessed us with every spiritual blessing."

Indeed, if we look into the Old Testament, we find that when Moses blessed the people, he blessed them much in temporal blessings. In Deuteronomy 28:2, Moses said, "And all these blessings shall come upon you and overtake you, because you obey the voice of the LORD your God." What are those blessings?

> Blessed shall you be in the city, and blessed shall you be in the country.
>
> Blessed shall be the fruit of your body, the produce of your ground and the increase of your herds, the increase of your cattle and the offspring of your flocks.
>
> Blessed shall be your basket and your kneading bowl. (Deut. 28:3–5)

Thus Moses named outward blessings.

But now if we look into the gospel and consider the blessings of Jesus Christ, and compare them with those of Moses, we shall find them to be spiritual blessings. In Matthew 5:3–4, Jesus said,

> Blessed are the poor in spirit,
> For theirs is the kingdom of heaven.

Blessed are those who mourn,
For they shall be comforted.

True, the promise of the earth comes in verse 5, but
then He returns again to spiritual blessings:

Blessed are those who hunger and thirst for
    righteousness,
For they shall be filled....
Blessed are the pure in heart,
For they shall see God. (vv. 6, 8)

These are spiritual blessings. This is the stream of
the gospel; it runs this way. When the Lord blesses a
person, He gives that which is suitable to that person. In
the times of the gospel, men are more spiritual than they
were in the times of the law; therefore gospel blessings
are spiritual blessings.

A thing gives and communicates to others according
to what it has itself. The sun communicates light to the
world because it itself has light. Parents communicate
human nature to their child because they themselves
have human nature. So it is with our Lord Christ.
When He blesses, He communicates according to what
He Himself has, and His blessings especially consist in
spiritual things. Indeed, in the Old Testament, by virtue of the covenant that was made with Abraham, there
were spiritual blessings mixed with temporal blessings.
In like manner now, outward blessings are thrown in
as extras with spiritual blessings. Nevertheless, though

these outward blessings are not spiritual in their nature, they are given with a spiritual end in view. Therefore, it is true to say that the blessing of Christ and the gospel is a spiritual blessing.

But more particularly, if you ask me in what this blessing consists, I shall name but two things. First, the blessing of Christ and the gospel first consists in supernatural, spiritual enjoyment of God in Christ—the love and favor of God in Christ. When the priests pronounced a blessing in the times of the Old Testament, in Numbers 6, they said:

> The LORD bless you and keep you;
> The LORD make His face shine upon you,
> And be gracious to you;
> The LORD lift up His countenance upon you,
> And give you peace. (vv. 24–26)

The apostle Paul, expounding this in 2 Corinthians 13:14, rendered it this way: "The grace of the Lord Jesus Christ, and the love of God, and the communion of the Holy Spirit be with you all. Amen." The Old Testament blessing had three parts: the Lord bless you, the Lord make His face to shine upon you, the Lord lift up His countenance upon you—three times, "the Lord, the Lord, the Lord," thus noting the Trinity. The apostle explained it here as the Father, the Son, and the Holy Spirit.

Or consider these words from Christ: "Blessed are the pure in heart, for they shall see God" (Matt. 5:8). To see God is a gospel blessing spoken by Christ. And what is it for a man to see God? In the Old Testament, the Hebrew word translated *to see* can mean "to enjoy." For example, Psalm 4:6, "Who will show us any good?" in Hebrew is, "Who will make us to see any good?" The meaning is, "Who will cause to enjoy any good?" So then to see God is to enjoy Him. When Jacob enjoyed God, he saw Him, and the place was called Peniel, for he had seen the Lord and there the Lord blessed him (Gen. 32:30). But we cannot see God except in Christ. Therefore, I say the blessing of the gospel consists in this—a supernatural and spiritual enjoyment of God in Christ, or in other words, the favor and love of God in Christ.

Second, the blessing also consists of the inhabitation of the Holy Spirit in our hearts—the gift of the Holy Spirit to the hearts of men. Therefore, Paul's blessing in 2 Corinthians 13:14 concludes with "and the communion of the Holy Spirit be with you all. Amen." That which is promised in the gospel must be the great blessing of Christ and the gospel. And what was promised? If we look in Acts 1:4–5, we read that the disciples should wait in Jerusalem for "the Promise of the Father." And what was this promise? The gift of the Holy Spirit.

In the Old Testament, the great promise was the gift of the Son, the coming of the second person. So, after Christ came, the great promise was the coming of the third person, the gift of the Holy Spirit. Christ said that when He departed He would send another Helper and that of "He who believes…out of his heart will flow rivers of living water" (see John 7:38; 14:16; 16:7). Christ said this concerning the Spirit, who had not yet been given in those extraordinary outpourings of gifts and graces, because Christ was not yet glorified. So then, the great gospel blessing that was to be given to His people was the Holy Spirit. This is a gospel blessing indeed.

What then does Christ do when He blesses us?

First, observe that when a superior blessed his inferior, as when a father blessed his child, he saw the greatest good and the choicest mercy of that time and wished it to him. For example, when Isaac blessed Jacob, the choice mercy was "the dew of heaven" (Gen. 27:28). So it is now when our Lord Jesus, our Great High Priest, blesses anyone. Seeing that the choice mercies of the gospel are our enjoyment of God in Christ (the favor and love of God), and the giving of the Holy Spirit into a person's heart, this is the good that Christ wishes upon us. So, when He prays to God the Father, He says, "Lord, let this poor soul have Thy favor. Oh, cause Thy face to shine upon this poor soul and give Thy Holy Spirit so that this person may walk after the Spirit."

In the second place, observe that when the priests blessed the people, they didn't merely wish good on them, but they authoritatively pronounced them blessed.

"So they shall put My name on the children of Israel, and I will bless them" (Num. 6:27). So when the Lord Christ, our Great High Priest, blesses a person, He does not merely wish this person good and He doesn't merely wish for God to shine His face upon this soul. Rather, when Christ blesses, being the High Priest, He authoritatively pronounces such a soul to be blessed.

Third, when the priest blessed, he not only pronounced the people blessed, but he did so with a kind of binding power. His blessing had the power, force, and efficacy of an absolution. Just as Christ said to His disciples, "If you forgive the sins of any, they are forgiven them; if you retain the sins of any, they are retained" (John 20:23). So the Lord said in Numbers 6:27: "So they shall put My name on the children of Israel, and I will bless them." The Lord stood by them in pronouncing the blessing. Therefore, when the Lord Jesus Christ, our Great High Priest, blesses, He not only pronounces a person to be blessed, but He absolves that person from all sin, and says, "By the authority that is given to Me by the Father and the keys that are put into My hand, I bind this blessing upon this poor soul."

Furthermore, when the priest blessed, though he could wish well and could pronounce someone blessed and pronounce absolution, he could go no further. He could not actually confer the blessing. But when our Lord Christ blesses—since He is a greater High Priest than any who ever came before Him—He not only pronounces the blessing, He also confers it. Being both God and man, He actually bestows the blessing.

Then, fifth, look how God blesses. Since our Great High Priest is both God and man, He blesses as God. In the Scriptures you will find that when God the Father blessed, He said to those things that He blessed, "Be fruitful and multiply" (Gen. 1:28). And when the Lord Jesus Christ as our High Priest blesses us, He does not merely wish good to a poor soul or pronounce a blessing or bestow a good thing upon a person, but He says, "O soul, be fruitful in this good; the Lord multiply your graces and gifts and comforts." This is what the Lord Christ our Great High Priest does. And so it is clear what the blessing of the gospel is, wherein it consists, and what our High Priest does when He blesses the people.

Made a Curse in Order to Bless

Second, does it especially belong to Jesus Christ to bless His people? Yes, for He was made a curse for sin. He—no one else—was made a curse for sin; therefore, it belongs to Him, above all the world, to bless. Look at the evil that Jesus Christ endured, the contrary good He merited for the children of men, and His power to bestow that good. Now He above all was cursed; He hung upon the cross and died a cursed death. He was made a curse; therefore, it belongs to Him above all to give the blessing to bless poor sinners.

The first in every kind is the cause of the rest. The sun is the cause of all the light we have here below, and it is the first body of light. And the Lord Jesus Christ is the first blessing; therefore, God has blessed you forever. In the Scriptures, we read of three kinds of people who especially blessed others: a father, a king, and a priest. A father blesses his children, a king blesses his subjects, and a priest blesses the people. Now the Lord Jesus Christ is our father—"Everlasting Father" (Isa. 9:6), our king—"I have set My King on My holy hill" (Ps. 2:6)—and our Great High Priest. Therefore all these relations meet in Christ, and it belongs to Him above all others to bless the people.

Christ's Great Willingness to Bless

Is the Lord Jesus Christ willing and inclined to bless poor sinners? Yes, He is very willing. He is much inclined toward and greatly delights in this work of blessing the people. Consider therefore what an abundance of blessings Christ scattered among the people when He was here upon the earth. You never read that He cursed any man. Once, indeed, He pronounced a curse, but it fell upon a barren fig tree, not upon a man. Take your Bibles and turn page after page to see how frequent He was to bless and consider whether you have read in all the Bible of any preacher or prophet who ever in their preaching pronounced as many blessings as did Christ: "Blessed are the poor," and "Blessed are those who mourn," and

"Blessed are those who hunger and thirst," and "Blessed are those who are persecuted for righteousness' sake," and "Blessed are those who hear the word of God and keep it" (Matt. 5:3–4, 6, 10; Luke 11:28). He took little children into His arms and blessed them. Mark in all the Gospels how frequent Christ was in blessing but never in cursing. There was never a preacher more frequent in blessing in his sermons. What is the reason for this? Because the Lord Jesus Christ, our High Priest, greatly delights in this work of blessing the people. It is a work to which He is most inclined.

Discerning Christ's Blessing

Does Christ actually do this work of blessing? Yes, He does, and He does it fully. The same passage that I quoted earlier will prove it—Ephesians 1:3: "Blessed be the God and Father of our Lord Jesus Christ, who has blessed us with every spiritual blessing in the heavenly places in Christ." The Father blesses us not only through the merits of Christ but by the hand of Christ. He has blessed us with all spiritual blessings, and He has done it in and by Jesus Christ.

You might say, "We do not see that people are thus blessed by Christ, for where Christ blesses, He does not only wish well and good to a person but also bestows it. Indeed, He does not only bestow good but increases and multiplies blessing. But upon this account, how few there are in the world who are blessed by Christ!"

To answer, it is sometimes difficult for a Christian to discern the blessing of Christ. You can see the branches, fruit, trunk, and bark of a tree, but to see the root, you have to dig. It is easy to see the leaves, but you must take pains to dig and see the root. The blessing of Jesus Christ is the root of all, and to see it, you must take pains to dig. It doesn't lie open to everyone's view. The Lord Jesus Christ, our High Priest, does not bless as man blesses. His blessing is very much hidden from our eyes. He does not bless as we do, as the world does. If the world sees a rich person, it pronounces that person blessed. "Oh, there is a blessed man!" or "There is a happy woman! What an excellent house she has, how abundantly is her table spread," etc. The world sees rich people and pronounces them happy and blessed. But our Lord Jesus Christ does as Jacob did when Joseph brought his two sons to him to be blessed. Joseph set Ephraim the younger on Jacob's left hand, and Manasseh the elder on his right hand, so that Jacob would give the right hand of blessing to the elder and the left hand to the younger. But when Joseph had thus set them before Jacob, Jacob crossed his hands and gave the right hand of blessing to the younger (Gen. 48:13–14).

So imagine two men are brought before Christ: a rich man and a poor man. In the eyes of the world, the rich man should get the blessing. Oh, but our Lord Christ crosses His hands, and often lays the blessing upon the younger brother! It is so in regard to ordinances. Two sorts of ordinances are brought before Christ: God's ordinance and man's ordinance. In the eyes of the world, man's ordinance is the elder brother and God's ordinance is the younger brother. And both are brought before Christ for a blessing, but the Lord Christ crosses His hands and lays the blessing upon the younger in this respect. So two men are brought before him: a proud Pharisee and a poor, brokenhearted sinner. The Pharisee comes to the right hand of Christ and thinks he will be given the blessing. But the Lord Christ crosses His hands and lays the right hand of blessing upon the poor, brokenhearted sinner, while passing by the proud Pharisee. The Lord Christ does not bless as the world blesses.

Second, as He does not bless as the world blesses, so He does not bless always as some professors bless. Professors ordinarily bless people according to their outward privileges, their gospel and church privileges. As the woman said to Christ, "Blessed is the womb that bore You, and the breasts which nursed You!" (Luke 11:27). But Christ essentially crossed His hands and said, "More than that, blessed are those who hear the word of God and keep it!" (v. 28). We bless according to outward privileges. But Christ does not go that way of blessing. He does not bless as professors bless.

Third, He does not always bless as godly, gracious men bless. For you who are godly pronounce a person blessed who has much grace, who has assurance of the love of God in Christ. You pronounce blessed the one who has strong and great gifts, one who is able to remember whole sermons word for word, who has strong memories and large gifts, who is head and shoulders above others. But though you pronounce those who have much grace and assurance as blessed, Christ does not always bless like this. "Blessed are the poor in spirit.... Blessed are those who mourn," He said. He did not say, "Blessed are those who rejoice" or "Blessed are those who have the assurance of God's love" or "Blessed are those who are strong in grace." But the Lord essentially said, "Do you know a poor, weak Christian, a mourning soul, who is like a dove in the valleys? That person is blessed."

I say, therefore, that the Lord Jesus Christ, our Great High Priest, does not bless as we bless. He does not bless as the world blesses. He does not bless always as professors bless. He does not bless always as godly men bless. Therefore, it is no wonder that His blessing is hidden. When children are very young, two or three years old, they are often blessed by their parents, though they do not take notice of it. So it is with many gracious souls who are blessed by Jesus Christ: they do not take notice of their Father's blessing.

The Lord Christ always blesses His people, but there are several special times and seasons in which He gives out His blessing. Let me briefly describe those times to you so that you may look for His blessing while His hand is hidden, as it were, so that you may be crowned with spiritual blessings in and from Jesus Christ.

First, when Christ our High Priest sees people weak in grace or gifts and has some work or service for them to do, some employment to call them to, then the Lord Christ blesses them. There are two times especially, as I remember, that the Lord said to mankind, "Be fruitful and multiply." Once in the beginning in Genesis 1, when He had made man and woman; and once in Genesis 9, when He had brought Noah out of the ark. Why did He choose to say "Be fruitful and multiply" at these two times, rather than at any other time? In the beginning, there was but a little stock of mankind, and the Lord purposed to make use of men and women in the world, and therefore He said, "Be fruitful and multiply." Afterward, when the flood had swept away men and women, Noah and his family had been preserved and came out of the ark. And the Lord having yet a further purpose for Noah and mankind, repeated those words again, "Be fruitful and multiply." So when the Lord Christ sees that people's hearts are upright and sincere, and He has some work and service for them to do, then the Lord comes forth and blesses them: "Oh soul, be fruitful and multiply, increase in your gifts and graces, and multiply." That is one time or season for blessing.

Second, as the Lord blesses weak gifts and graces when He intends to use them, so also when He uses people for His work, then the Lord blesses them. When Abraham had done a great work, slaying the kings and rescuing Lot, then Melchizedek the High Priest, that great type of Christ, came forth and blessed him. So when the Lord Jesus Christ our Great High Priest sees poor souls have been at His work and service and have done their work faithfully, then Christ comes forth and blesses those souls: "O soul, live forever!"

Third, as the Lord blesses people when they have done His work, so also He blesses people when they are willing to leave all their family and natural engagements to follow Him and to cling close to Him, His ways, and His ordinances. So the Lord blessed Abraham, saying,

> I will bless you
> And make your name great;
> And you shall be a blessing. (Gen. 12:2)

What was the occasion? The Lord had said to Abraham,

> Get out of your country,
> From your family
> And from your father's house,
> To a land that I will show you. (Gen. 12:1)

And Abraham did so. He pulled up his tent and went after the Lord, leaving his own family, and then the Lord blessed him. So also, when the Lord Christ our High Priest sees people willing to leave their family in order to follow Him, willing to leave all their natural engagements in order to be His servant, then the Lord Christ comes and says, "These souls I bless; in blessing

I will bless you, and I will bless you greatly." That is a
third time when Christ blesses.

Fourth, the Lord Christ, our High Priest, blesses
when the world curses. A special time of Christ's blessing is when the world curses. When Rabshakeh reviled,
blasphemed, and cursed, then God blessed (2 Kings
18–19). When Balak hired Balaam to curse the people
of Israel, then the Lord blessed them by the mouth of
Balaam himself (Numbers 22–23). Christ spoke about
this in Matthew 5:10, "Blessed are those who are persecuted for righteousness' sake." But when are they
blessed? "Blessed are you when they revile and persecute you, and say all kinds of evil against you falsely for
My sake" (v. 11). Yes, but suppose it does not come to
bodily persecution. Men may not be thrown in prison
or brought to the stake. But Jesus Christ said, "Blessed
are you when they revile...you"—when they persecute
you with the tongue—"and say all kinds of evil against
you falsely for My sake." When the world says that poor
souls are hypocrites and says all manner of evil that can
be devised against them for the name of Christ, that is
the very time when Christ comes to bless those souls. It
is a blessed season.

Fifth, the Lord Christ also blesses when His people
graciously enjoy the ordinances purely and evangelically
administered. It is said concerning Zion,

> Blessed are the people who know the joyful
> sound!

They walk, O LORD, in the light of Your
countenance. (Ps. 89:15)

For there the LORD commanded the blessing—
Life forevermore. (Ps. 133:3)

It is written in the Old Testament that the priests blessed the people when they came together. When the people came together to enjoy the ordinances according to God's own appointment, then the priests blessed them. If their high priest blessed them then, shall not our High Priest bless us now? The priests blessed who sat under the Mosaic ordinances, so shall our High Priest bless the people who sit under evangelical and gospel ordinances, purely and evangelically administered. The people then could give account of the greatest blessing, and so also you may give account of the blessing of Jesus Christ when you enjoy ordinances. But there is this difference (there are other differences, too, but I'll only speak of this one)—in the Old Testament, the priests blessed the people when the congregation was dismissed; but now, the Lord Jesus Christ, our Great High Priest, blesses them the whole time. He goes up and down as the word is preached and the ordinances administered, blessing the souls as they sit longing for Him and sighing after Him. He is blessing them the whole time.

Therefore, the Lord does bless. Though you do not always perceive it, yet He blesses His people.

Our Comfort and Holiness

Does all this lead to our comfort and our holiness? Yes, much in every way.

Comfort

Beloved, is it not comforting to be blessed by Jesus Christ? Children counted it a great matter to be blessed by their parents. After Jacob got the blessing from Esau, Esau sat down and mourned; he could not be comforted because the blessing was gone. And Jacob, though he was thrust out of doors, yet he went away cheerful because he had gotten the blessing—and this was but Isaac's blessing. But behold a greater than Isaac is here! Oh, it was good to have Isaac's blessing! So it is even greater to be blessed by Jesus Christ. Beloved! When Christ blesses, He turns all our curses into blessings and all our miseries into mercies. When God curses, He turns our table into a snare (Ps. 69:22); but when Christ blesses, He turns our snare into a table. In Genesis 49:4–7 Jacob pronounced a curse upon his two sons, Simeon and Levi, that they should be divided and scattered in Israel. Afterward, the tribe of Levi stood up at the commandment of God to execute justice and judgment, and the Lord blessed them. How did He bless them? They were to be the preachers to all the tribes; in order that they might be preachers to all the tribes, they were to be scattered into all the tribes—so Jacob's curse was turned into a blessing to them.

It is comforting for people's curses to become blessings. But it is also comforting for people to have all those who curse them become those who bless them. When the Lord Christ blesses, He will make those who curse whether they will or not (in the day of their visitation at least) to bless. You know that Balaam would have cursed Israel, but the Lord had blessed them. Balaam went upon a high mountain, from which he would have cursed Israel, but it would not be. Then he went upon another high mountain, from which he would have cursed Israel, but it would not be. Then he went upon another high mountain, thinking that would have done it, and from there he would have cursed Israel, but that would not do it. Oh, he said, the Lord "has not observed iniquity in Jacob" (Num. 23:21), and therefore, he blessed them. The curse was turned into a blessing. So there are many who deal thus with the people of God in these days—they go upon a high mountain, such a great and high means, and think to curse the people of God from there, but it will not be. Then they get upon another mountain, another means, thinking to curse the people of God from there, but it will not be. Then they get upon another high mountain or hill, and think then to curse the people of God and do them mischief, but it will not be. Why? For the Lord Christ sees no iniquity, so the Lord Christ has blessed them. And so at last, in the day of their visitation, the wicked are forced to say, "These are the people of God;

they are blessed and shall be blessed." We know what is said in Scripture,

> The blessing of the LORD makes one rich,
> And He adds no sorrow with it. (Prov. 10:22)

Is it not a good thing then to be blessed by Christ? If people are blessed by Jesus Christ, they may bless themselves in the Lord, comfort themselves in every condition, and say, "Well, though we are a poor people, yet we are blessed by Christ. Though our estate is lost and decayed, yet we are blessed by Christ; and though we are reproached and hated by men, yet we are blessed by Jesus Christ." So people may comfort themselves in every condition.

But you might say, "Indeed, if you are assured that Christ has blessed you, then you can comfort yourself in this way. But I am afraid that Christ has not blessed me or that He is not willing to bless me. If I could be assured that this Great High Priest had once laid His hand of blessing upon me, I would have comfort in all conditions."

Let me present two or three things to you concerning this. First, when the Lord blessed Abraham, He said to him, "In you and in your seed shall all the nations of the earth be blessed" (see Gen. 12:3; 22:18). Others being blessed through Abraham was a sign to him that he was blessed. So now, when a person's gifts, graces, and comforts are blessings to others, it is an argument that that person is blessed.

Further, when people are blessed by God, they are drawn nearer to God by all things. "Come, you blessed…. Depart from Me you cursed" (Matt. 25:34, 41). Blessing has an attracting quality. "*Come* you blessed" (emphasis added). When the Lord Christ blesses people, he also draws those people to Himself. When a person is brought nearer to God by affliction, that person is blessed. When a person is brought nearer to God by any comfort or by any sorrow, that is a blessing. "Come, you blessed." Blessings draw one nearer to God with a cord of love.

Third, where the Lord blesses, He causes people to increase and multiply in that thing in which they have been blessed. Increasing and multiplying is so natural to blessing that in the original tongues of the Old and New Testaments, the idea of plenty means blessing. I will give you one clear place for it in the New Testament: "Therefore I thought it necessary to exhort the brethren, that they would go before unto you, and make up beforehand your bounty [blessing] whereof ye had notice before, that the same might be ready, as a matter of bounty" (2 Cor. 9:5 KJV). The word *bounty* is actually blessing. But especially see the next verse: "But this I say, He which soweth sparingly shall reap also sparingly; and he which soweth bountifully shall reap also bountifully" (v. 6 KJV). That is, "he which soweth with blessing" (as it is in the original) "shall reap with blessing." And here blessing is opposed to "sparingly," and translated "bountifully." So, when the Lord blesses, He always causes a person to increase and multiply.

Now, beloved in the Lord, I appeal to all your souls, you who make this objection, who are afraid that the Lord Christ has not blessed you as your High Priest and has not laid His hand upon you and blessed you. Do you not yet know more of Christ than you knew before? Have the hidden things of the gospel increased and multiplied in your hearts? And haven't your hearts been brought nearer to God by affliction? Haven't your souls been drawn nearer to God by His outward dealings with you? And as Abraham was blessed because he was made a blessing to others, so I appeal to you, have not your gifts and graces, in some measure, been a blessing to others? Even to your poor family and to others also? Then be of good comfort, man or woman— wherever you stand, the Lord has blessed you, and you shall be blessed. Hold up your head, you poor blessed soul. The Lord Jesus has blessed you. When the Lord laid His blessing upon you, I cannot tell you, but I do find you to be a blessed person. So, stay yourself upon the Lord and cheer up your drooping heart. You are a blessed soul.

Holiness

But you might say, "How does this lead to our holiness? I confess this is a very comforting medicine, that the Lord Jesus Christ is in office to bless poor sinners, but how does this lead to our holiness?"

It does so greatly. For it holds forth great encouragement to all poor sinners to come to Christ and to come without delay. Why? Those who come to Christ are blessed, but those without Christ are cursed. If you are an enemy to Jesus Christ, then you are a cursed person: cursed in your storehouse, cursed in your basket, and cursed in all things that you set your hand to. Oh, then, will you not come to Christ that you may be blessed? The day poor souls come to Christ, whatever they may have been, they are blessed. That day may be called Gilgal, for then the curse is rolled away from him.

Blessed is he whose transgression is forgiven,
Whose sin is covered. (Ps. 32:1)

The first day—the first minute—that they come to Christ, their sins are pardoned, and they are blessed. Who would not then come to Christ now, that they may be blessed forever? When Esau sold his birthright for a stew of lentils, the Lord looked upon him as a profane man. And he stands upon record in Scripture as an example of a profane man to this day, because he sold his birthright. And the text says, "For you know that afterward, when he wanted to inherit the blessing, he was rejected, for he found no place for repentance, though he sought it diligently with tears" (Heb. 12:17).

The Lord Jesus Christ is now among us and offers to bless us. But if I would rather keep my sins than come to Jesus Christ, the Lord will look upon me as a profane

man, and I may go and seek the blessing with tears and
never recover it again. If ever a drunkard or swearer or
immoral and unclean wanton reads this book, mind what
is said for your everlasting peace. Oh, here is something
that should make every wicked man to look upon the
godly as David did upon the swallows that made their
nests in the altar (Ps. 84:3). David envied the birds that
had a place at the altar to nest and sing, while he was
kept at a distance. Thus he was provoked by the sparrows
and swallows making their nests near the altar. And so
a wicked person should say, "There are godly people,
indeed. They can go to Jesus Christ in prayer. They can
offer up their gift to God the Father by the hands of
Christ. They can come near to God through Christ. But
as for me, I am without Christ. I have not yet gone to
Jesus Christ. I am a cursed swearer. I am such a profane
drunkard. I am such a vile, wretched, immoral person,
such a notorious, scandalous sinner! Oh, these people
are blessed, but I am cursed! But now through the Lord's
grace, I will go to the Lord Christ that I may be blessed."

Yes, my beloved. Here, I believe, is a strong invitation
to all young people to come to Jesus Christ, even those
who are very young. Hear the word of the Lord, you children. The Lord Jesus Christ received children into His
arms and blessed them. You who are nine, ten, eleven,
twelve, thirteen, fourteen, or fifteen years old, you can be
concerned for your father's blessing and have often gone
down upon your knees to your father, saying, "Pray, my

father; pray to God to bless me." Oh, will you go to your earthly father for his blessing but not go to Jesus Christ? He is an everlasting Father (Isa. 9:6). This your earthly father will be dead before long, but Christ is an everlasting Father. Children, He is willing and able to bless you. Have you gone down upon your knees to your earthly father? Oh, children, go down, down upon your knees before the Lord Jesus Christ! Go to Him for His blessing. Some of you, perhaps, have never gone to Christ for His blessing. You have lived so many years—ten, eleven, or twelve years—and all this time, you have never gone to Christ as your High Priest for His blessing. Oh, what a mighty encouragement is here for all people to come to Christ that they might be blessed by Him!

Further, as there is an encouragement to come to Christ, so this argument also encourages us to go on in the good ways of Christ, notwithstanding all the opposition that we meet along the way. I say, it encourages us to go on in the face of all opposition. For when Abraham went to battle, then Melchizedek the High Priest came to bless him. And when a poor soul goes out to battle for Christ, then comes our great Melchizedek, our Great High Priest Jesus Christ, to bless that soul. The time of opposition is the time of Christ's blessing. Therefore, why should I allow opposition to discourage me or beat me out of the way of Christ, though the opposition is never so great? Times of opposition are Christ's time for blessing.

Again, this argument not only speaks encouragement against all opposition but it also encourages us to go on in the good ways of God when we are called to them, though we are weak and have but little strength. Though there is but little oil in the jar and though there is but little food in the barrel, if Christ calls a person to the work, He will bless the person in it. And when Christ blesses, He multiplies and increases a person's gifts as they are used. When He commanded the people to sit down and eat, He also multiplied and increased the bread in their eating. So now, does Christ call me to any work or service? Well then, though I am weak, though I do not have enough oil or food, though I do not have enough strength, yet the Lord Christ will bless. And when He blesses, He increases and multiplies. Why should I not, therefore, go on in His work, if He calls me to it, though I have but little strength?

Furthermore, if all this is true, why should not a man be content in his condition, though it is never so small? Beloved in the Lord! Is there not enough in Christ's blessing? Truly, anyone whom Christ's blessing will not satisfy is too covetous. Well, whatever my condition is, yet I may be blessed by Jesus Christ. Has the Lord blessed me? Then I will be content with my condition, even if it is small. As Jacob once said, "I have all things."

Yes, and in the fifth and last place, here is that which if well studied and considered will provoke us all to continually bless the Lord! What is the life of a Christian here but a continual blessing from God? It is heaven begun. And in heaven, they do nothing but bless and praise the Lord. I say, then, that our life here is heaven begun, and therefore a Christian should be always blessing and praising the Lord. But what will make a person to be always blessing and praising God in Christ? The knowledge that a person is blessed by Christ will make a person bless God for Christ. Consider how the apostle reasons, in Ephesians 1:3, "Blessed be the God and Father of our Lord Jesus Christ." Why is He blessed? The rest of the verse says—"who has blessed us." Once people can come to this, to say that the Lord Christ has blessed them, then they will break forth into blessing and praising the Lord. Oh, blessed be the Lord! Bless the Lord, Oh my soul, and bless the Lord all that is within me, for the Lord has blessed me with spiritual blessings. Do you therefore desire to be always in this work of blessing the Lord? Then think much of this.

Conclusion

To conclude, let me remind you of all you have read. You have read that it is the work of our Great High Priest to make satisfaction for the sins of the people, to answer all the accusations that are brought against them, to offer up all their prayers and gifts to God the Father, and to bless these poor souls.

Now then, beloved, according to all your wants and according to all your temptations, I beseech you in the Lord, go to Jesus Christ, to this High Priest. Try to see if you do not find it true, that the Lord makes all of this good to you. If you are suffering any spiritual want or temptation, put before your soul the alternatives. Say, "Come, oh my soul; either the Lord Jesus Christ is our Great High Priest, or else He is not. If He is not, what do these Scriptures mean? If the Lord Jesus Christ is our High Priest, then surely He will be faithful and do all the work of a High Priest for my soul. Indeed, I have sinned and sinned greatly. But, oh Lord, it is the work of our High Priest to offer satisfaction for sin. Now, Lord Jesus, I come to you as my High Priest. Oh, satisfy for me! Indeed, I confess my own conscience accuses me, Satan accuses me, and Moses accuses me. But it is the work of our Great High Priest to take all of the accusations that are brought against poor believers. Lord, I now come to You as my Great High Priest. Oh, take away this accusation that my poor soul labors under! Indeed, when I look upon my own duties, there is so much deadness, so much hardness of heart, and so many distractions that accompany them that I am afraid they will never be accepted. But, oh Lord, it is the work of our Great High Priest to take away the weeds of the duty and to present the duty. Oh Lord, I now come to You as my High Priest. Oh, carry my prayers into the presence of God the Father! Yes, when I look upon my former life, Lord, I cannot but conclude myself to be a poor cursed sinner. But notwithstanding, it is the work of our Great High Priest to bless the people. Oh Lord, I therefore now come to You as my High Priest. Oh, bless me, and say to all my graces, "Be fruitful and multiply!"